From Ramen to Riches™
Finding a Job in Your 20s

A Young Professional's Guide to Career Search,
Networking, Resume Writing, Interviewing, and
Succeeding at Work

LAUREN S. TANNY

JAMES G. WOOD

The authors welcome feedback to improve future editions. Due to the volume of mail they receive, the authors regret that they will be unable to respond individually to every message.

This book is sold with the understanding that the contents herein are for general information and may not be suitable for your specific situation. If expert advice is required, please consult with a competent professional. While the author and publisher have used their best efforts in preparing this book, they disclaim any liability with respect to the accuracy or completeness of the information.

ISBN 978-0-9828251-2-9

Library of Congress Control Number: 2012917646
Library of Congress subject headings:
Job hunting.
Vocational guidance.
Job satisfaction.

Cover image and design by Incitrio, San Diego, California.

Published by
The Tannywood Group, Inc.
San Diego, California
Contact: publishing@tannywood.com
www.tannywood.com

DEDICATION

For our parents,

who taught us to work hard and do our best.

CONTENTS

ACKNOWLEDGMENTS

Many friends and colleagues generously contributed their expertise and real-life experiences to this effort. Among them are current and former managers, executives, and other experts. They include Megan Ahn, Mindy Bortness, Kim Box, Rebecca Castleton, Diane Gallo, Jeff Hastings, Susan Penn, Sherri Petro, Rhonda Rhyne, Ken Schmitt, Cláudia Schwartz, Mark Title, and Barbara Wakefield. They are all consummate professionals and we are deeply grateful for their insights, wisdom, and support.

We also want to acknowledge several people who read early editions of the manuscript and provided very helpful comments and feedback. Thanks to Hilary Babon, Mike Cesaro, Stacy Christensen, Patsy Murphy, Susan Penn, Diane Rosenblum, Greg Sabbatini, Marilyn Tanny, and Nick Wetta.

Lastly, we owe a special debt of gratitude to four people who went through the early editions with a fine-tooth comb and provided an incredibly detailed level of feedback on our content. They are: Robert Strauss, Mark Title, Tricia Whittemore, and Katherine Willey. Thank you for volunteering your sharp minds and eyes!

We are so grateful and privileged to have you all in our lives.

CHAPTER 1

INTRODUCTION

"Far and away the best prize that life has to offer
is the chance to work hard at work worth doing."
- THEODORE ROOSEVELT

Working in a rewarding job is one of life's greatest joys. Contributing in a meaningful way to something you care about and being compensated fairly for your efforts generates a wonderful sense of satisfaction and happiness in your life. Finding a job you love requires really knowing yourself: what makes you tick, what inspires you, what excites you. You may be further down that path than we were in our 20s. At the time, we cared more about moving from the small towns where we grew up to sunny California than we did about finding work that fed our souls. We didn't even know that our souls wanted to be fed.

Over time, doing work we really cared about became more important. We began to acquire a deeper understanding of where we wanted to take our lives and the role that our work would play in that quest. Now in our 50s, we finally love what we do. While we've chosen work that pays less than our earlier corporate gigs, we are actually happier. We want you to find work that feeds your soul at the beginning of your career. This book will show you how.

While the information that follows is relevant for anyone looking to find a job or switch careers, we have aimed the material at young professionals who are early in their working lives. Most people in their 20s have the energy, enthusiasm, and commitment to embark on a quest for career fulfillment. Take advantage of it!

Our intention is to help you find work you love way sooner than we did. We will share some of the experiences we and others have had in moving to work that's more rich, joyful, and fulfilling than what came before. After you finish reading, will the heavens open up and your ideal job magically appear with a lotto-sized paycheck? Probably not. Finding a dream job is a process, not an event. It takes effort. We will set you on the road to understanding how a successful job search works, how to identify your skills and interests, and how to find a position that's a good fit for you.

In our own journeys, each career move we've made has brought us closer to work that feels like a great fit with who we are and still pays the bills. You may be one of the rare individuals who has known exactly what you wanted to do since you were a kid. If so, fantastic! For most people though, the journey requires experiencing what works and what doesn't. In short, the process is one of discovery.

So Why Listen to Us?

At various times over the last 30 years, we've been in the same boat you're in right now. We know what it feels like to be looking for a first job or a better one while figuring out how to pay the bills. Over the years, we arrived at points in our careers where we wondered, "Is this all there is? How can I contribute more to the world and still draw an awesome paycheck?" We've dealt with our own work-related ups and downs: the petty politics, occasionally the incompetent boss, but also the joys of bringing something important to completion, contributing to a mission we believe in, and loving what we do.

Early in our careers, we both lived the lives of corporate cubicle dwellers. Jim started as a software engineer after graduating from Boston University. He then spent many years in middle management at a large multinational high-tech firm prior to becoming an author and entrepreneur. In Lauren's case, she held individual contributor and management positions with major insurance companies following her graduation from Dartmouth College. After earning an MBA from Stanford University, her positions steadily grew into executive management of publicly traded companies and start-ups in a variety of industries before she started her own consulting firm.

In her current incarnation, Lauren is an executive coach who helps senior leaders become more effective at what they do. That role sometimes includes helping clients work through job and career transitions for themselves and members of their organizations. She is passionate about helping people at all levels find work that is fulfilling to them.

We've been interviewed and been the interviewers. Between us, we've probably seen more than 1,000 resumes. We've interviewed hundreds of people, hired dozens, and fired a few. In this book, we will share what we've learned from these experiences and what we've determined makes a successful job search: self-assessment, finding one's passions, and the process of mapping those interests to a fulfilling career. While there's no one right answer on how to go about it, we've done it enough ourselves and coached so many others that we believe we can make your process a bit easier in the pages that follow.

We also surveyed about a dozen experts and colleagues who we felt could offer job search advice to young professionals. These people include vice presidents of human resources, executive recruiters, middle and senior managers with extensive hiring experience, and several current or former CEOs. They have generously offered their unique insights that provide additional perspective on the job search process, tuned specifically to people early in their careers.

Keys to Success in a Job Search

Your task during job search is to find open positions that align with your skills and interests, and then become a finalist for as many as possible. In order, here are seven steps to do just that:

1. **Conduct a rigorous self-assessment**. If you really know who you are, what you're good at, what you care about, and what you want, you will distinguish yourself from the vast majority of job seekers of any age.

2. **Find your passion**. True passion can trump experience. Demonstrating passion as a job candidate carries a great deal of weight and can overcome other weaknesses.

3. **Clearly explain and leverage your experience**. You may not have exactly parallel experience to the job you want, but our guess is that you can find examples from your past that are relevant. Actual on-the-job experience is best, but even high school and college experiences count. Did you have a leadership role in any clubs? Did you distinguish yourself in a particular academic or extracurricular activity? Did you have summer jobs or internships that demonstrated responsibility, dedication, and motivation? You likely have a plethora of experiences that are relevant to your professional life. The trick is creating a comprehensive list of what you've done and thinking about how to position those experiences in a way that will impress a future employer.

4. **Identify your skills**. Throughout your life, you have honed many skills. You've acquired useful academic knowledge. You may have relevant work experience from paid employment or from internships. You've probably had the opportunity to develop teamwork and leadership abilities through sports, clubs, and group projects. The countless hours you may have

spent on hobbies, musical training, or the arts help develop a variety of special abilities that an employer would value. These and other examples of competencies you've acquired are relevant in the working world. Knowing how to convey them to a hiring manager is essential.

5. **Build a strong network**. Most jobs are found through networking, so that is where you will need to spend most of your time when job searching. Don't panic if your network isn't robust. You already know more people than you think you do. Through targeted and effective networking, you can build a strong and supportive group of people who can help you find a good job.

6. **Master the job search process**. A scattershot approach to finding a job will probably leave you feeling disappointed and unsuccessful. An organized and methodical search, with support from people who care about you, will greatly improve the odds of landing something you want. It'll also be much quicker.

7. **Embody the right attitude**. Job search is tough. We won't sugarcoat that. Employers are looking for people who can maintain a positive attitude in tough times. They are looking for employees who want to contribute to a company's growth and success, not those who are only looking at what they themselves can get from a company. "It's all about me," doesn't work in the job market. An upbeat, can-do attitude will serve you well not just during your search, but also as an employee. Does this mean plastering on a fake smile and sucking up? No. People will see through that. It also doesn't mean pretending to be happy when you're not. Everyone has a bad day from time to time. What we mean is that deep down to your core, you have an authentically enthusiastic attitude to life and to your work. Attitudes like that are infectious and people will want to be around you. And hire you.

The Ten Most Common Mistakes of Job Searches

In Lauren's coaching practice, she's worked with more than 100 career-transition clients at all levels of corporate and non-profit organizational structures. In helping people address their job searches, here are the typical mistakes she has seen:

1. Spending too little time and energy on self-assessment. This leads to lack of clarity on what you want, what you are a good fit for, and why. Thus, it's very hard for others to help you.
2. Approaching the job search with "shoulds" rather than "wants." For example, "I majored in finance, so I *should* take a job in that field." Focus on what you *want* to do, not what you *should* do.

3. Reaching out to your best contacts before you've figured out what you are looking for. You don't want to use up their precious goodwill before they can really help you.
4. Having too broad a target, be it industry, company, or job title. Specificity helps people help you.
5. Being reluctant to ask for help.
6. Asking contacts for job openings, rather than introductions or information.
7. Spending too much time responding to job openings on websites. The average response from employers via these channels is depressingly low. Even if you do get a response, the competition is fierce.
8. Under-preparing for job or informational interviews. With the availability of Internet research, there's no excuse!
9. Going for money over job fit and satisfaction.
10. Neglecting to look at the longer-term career implications of choosing a particular job, company, or industry.

By following a well-defined job search process, you'll avoid these common pitfalls and greatly improve the odds of landing a position you really want. It'll take less time and feel more empowering than a random approach filled with the potholes described above.

How to Use This Book

In the pages that follow, we take a comprehensive approach to laying out the entire job search process. We recognize that each reader is at a unique stage in his or her career and in the search process. We strongly encourage you to review the entire process that's outlined in the next chapter first, even if you need to skip ahead for an immediate need, such as preparing for an upcoming interview or responding to a request for an updated resume. You'll discover important steps often overlooked by job seekers that you don't want to miss.

To get maximum value, you'll be doing a variety of exercises throughout the book. We recommend that you dedicate a notebook (electronic or paper) to this purpose. It'll help you crystallize your thoughts on what you want and will help organize your search.

The same advice goes for your job search. As you'll soon discover, the best results will come from doing the work of understanding what you really want, and then building a network of people who will help you get it. Simply submitting online job applications in the comfort of your home won't work.

We wish you a pleasant journey with your job search. Looking for a job can be one of the most mind-expanding, friend-generating, flexible times in your life, if you make it so. The following pages will guide you down that path.

CHAPTER 2

JOB SEARCH PROCESS OVERVIEW

"Plaster thick, some will stick." – PROVERB

The job search process we'll share with you works well for most people. In Lauren's career coaching practice, she has guided many clients through the same steps as they work to define what they want and ultimately accept positions that align with their criteria.

Be aware that a job quest is not linear. You will go through several steps more than once. You will also be at different stages of the process on different opportunities, at the same time. This is particularly true once you begin networking and informational interviewing. As you discover more about what you like and learn about potential industries and job titles, you will return to earlier stages and refine your work to incorporate the new information.

The amount of time you'll spend in each part of the process will vary widely across individuals. You'll have control over certain components (defining what you want; constructing your resume; building your network; etc). Other parts, like phone screens and job interviews, will happen according to potential employers' timelines. Take control of the things you can manage. Learn to navigate through the parts you can't.

The chapters that follow will delve into each of these subjects in more detail. For now, we'd like you to internalize the typical sequence of events, milestones, and tasks that will take place as your search unfolds. If we chart this process, it would look something like this:

Job Search Process Overview

Read and Learn	Do	Result
Chapter 3-4: Your Life Vision; Career Strategy and Guidelines	Craft a Life Vision, career strategy, and goals	A big picture overview of what you want over the next 5-10 years
Chapter 5: Self-assessment	Clarify what you're good at and passionate about	1. Top five values, passions, and skills 2. 1-2 target jobs and industry combinations to explore
Chapter 6: Your Job Criteria	1. Discover and prioritize your ideal job criteria 2. Figure out what a job must have for you to even apply	Ideal job and must-have criteria lists
Chapter 7: Your Resume	Compile a resume targeted to the job and industry you want	Clear, well-articulated resume that presents you well to potential employers
Chapters 8-9: Networking and Informational Interviewing	1. Expand your current network to a broader one 2. Learn more about your target job and industry combinations	1. Narrow your focus to one job and industry combination 2. Specific job opportunities may start appearing
Chapter 10: Target Company List	Based on desired job and industry, research specific company possibilities	List of target companies for use in networking and at informational interviews

Job Search Process Overview (continued)

Read and Learn	Do	Result
Chapter 11: Sustaining Your Search	Add structure and rewards	1. Continually expanding network and knowledge 2. More specific job opportunities appear for you to pursue 3. Continued motivation and excitement
Chapter 12: Interviewing	Research and prepare well	1. Aced interviews! 2. Job offers! 3. Some "not a fit" decisions
Chapter 13: Negotiating and Choosing	Assess job offer(s) and negotiate the best package	1. Choose a job 2. Decline others
Chapter 14: After Acceptance	1. Inform others 2. Understand your benefits	1. Keep your network strong 2. Maximize the value of your package
Chapter 15: Your First Few Months on the Job	1. Navigate the waters of the new job 2. Build a successful track record	1. Great start to new job 2. Expanded network within industry

Let's take a high-level look at each of these key components of a successful job search.

The Big Picture

An important and often neglected part of job search is looking at how your career aspirations fit into the larger picture of what you want out of your life. How does your job mesh with lifestyle goals, relationships, dreams, and big life events? By constructing a Life Vision in Chapter 3, you'll have an inspiring and compelling narrative to describe what want your life to look like in the future. The completed document helps focus your actions in the present so that you take appropriate steps early in your career to move towards the picture described in your vision.

In Chapter 4, "Career Strategy," we've identified several guidelines that will help you translate the vision into a plan of action for defining your career strategy and locating a job. The output from this effort is a concise statement of where you want to go with your career over the next several years, along with a rough timeline containing major milestones and things you want to learn and accomplish.

Getting Your Act Together

Before you start sending out job search emails and making phone calls, you need to get focused and organized. A scattershot approach, where you're applying to every job that shows up, will ultimately be unproductive, exhausting, and self-defeating. Many people think they have to be broad and open in looking for their target job so they won't miss any opportunities. In what we call the "paradox of job search," it turns out that when you are more specific about what you want, people are better able to help you find it.

Here's a hypothetical example. You meet an acquaintance at a coffee shop one morning. The person says, "I'm looking for an entry level job at a good company." What is your reaction? (Ours might be something like, "Oh, sorry to hear you're still unemployed. We'll treat for the coffee.") So, while the acquaintance might get a free coffee out of his pitch, it's unlikely he'd get much help finding a job because the request is much too broad to bring something specific to mind.

Let's change the above scenario a bit. At the coffee shop, your acquaintance instead said, "I'm looking for an entry-level information technology job at a small web services company." Ah, much better. By being specific, people are better able to come up with names of people or companies.

Figuring out what you want takes time. You'll continually refine it during your search. Sometimes you may abandon one avenue altogether. (Did you ever switch majors in college?) Since you're new to the workforce, your wording may not be as precise as the example above. In one of Lauren's career changes, her description was, "I want to manage and motivate people in a company that offers a quality product or service." That summary eventually led her to a director-level sales position for a healthcare publisher.

Assess your values, identify things you're passionate about, profile your skills, and summarize your life and work experience to assist you in gaining clarity. This is the focus of Chapter 5. A rigorous self-assessment will crystallize those things you really like to do, highlight the topics you're passionate about, and define the values that are important to you. When exploring opportunities, you'll be more focused and better positioned to know whether you'll care about the work you'll be doing. It's no fun doing a job that makes you miserable. It's equally unpleasant to arrive at a new job and discover you don't fit in because you didn't adequately perform due diligence on the employer's work culture.

Similarly, by specifying your ideal job criteria in advance, you'll be clear about what you want and will be better able to evaluate employment offers. It's unlikely that the offers you get will be perfect, but a set of ranked criteria prepared in advance will ensure you have the essential components in place. Further, a set of must-have criteria will help you decide whether it is even worth applying to a particular opening in the first place. See Chapter 6 for more.

The final task in building your tool set is preparation of a resume that accurately highlights your skills, interests, and work/life experiences that are relevant to a future employer. A great resume may not get you in the door. However, you can be guaranteed that a poorly written resume will keep you out. You don't want to flub the introduction that this document makes for you. It will help convince a hiring manager to take the next step with you. Chapter 7 covers all the details.

Getting Out There

Your odds of obtaining a job by responding to online ads safely ensconced in your home are quite low. Most jobs are obtained through networking. To be successful, you will need to get out and meet people who will introduce you to people who will introduce you to someone who has a job opening. If you're an introvert, we know we just made your heart sink. Don't worry. In Chapter 8, we outline ways you can go about this task with a minimum of heartburn. Actually, we think you will even have some fun with it!

Your network will also provide you with resources to find out more about industries or jobs in which you have an interest. Commonly called informational interviewing, this is a great way to find out what work life is really like in your chosen field. It's also a handy way to discover what's going on in the industry and whether a company's culture maps to its picture-perfect website. This is the focus of Chapter 9.

As you talk to more people in your network and through informational interviews and research, you'll accumulate names of companies to add to your target list (see Chapter 10). These are the potential employers that meet your criteria, be it company culture, industry, product set, location, salary, benefits, and so on. Companies develop reputations in the communities in which they operate. Some firms develop a buzz as a great place to work. Other organizations are avoided by all but the clueless. The more people you talk with, the better you'll be able to assess how companies score against your desired traits. Information about culture is difficult to get by simply surfing online.

Making It Happen

Job search is not an easy process. Over a period of weeks or months, you need to put out a great deal of positive energy and confidence in the midst of occasional rejection. Organizing your approach, managing your time, and building in rewards and reinforcement are important components to sustaining your enthusiasm until the optimal offer materializes. It also helps to hang out with other job searchers who are upbeat and diligent. Chapter 11 has several ideas to help you through this.

At various points, you'll cycle through phone screens and formal job interviews. You'll get better with every successive interaction. You'll meet some great people and perhaps a few jerks. You'll learn a lot, whether or not an offer materializes. You'll see some amazing new ideas and products and will likely also run across places that will redefine the meaning of boring. In Chapter 12, we discuss the art of interviewing so that you are prepared and confident.

One or more of the interviews will result in a formal offer. Wow, what a great feeling that will be! How will you know whether or not to accept? Should you pounce on the first offer or wait until something better shows up? Is there any negotiating room in the package that's been offered? How might you handle a situation where more than one offer appears at roughly the same time?

The good news is that these scenarios are high-class problems. Since you won't even apply to firms that don't meet your minimum criteria, odds are good that you would be enthusiastic about accepting one of the jobs that are offered. (This presumes the companies haven't low-balled their offers or that something else doesn't smell bad.) Still, you want to negotiate the final deal to include terms that are as favorable as possible. In the happy case of multiple offers, it helps to have a set of criteria to weigh one against the other so you choose the one that optimizes all your desired characteristics. Chapter 13 demonstrates how you can powerfully approach this decision.

Once You Accept

Once you formally accept an offer, your job search is technically finished. However, you'll still need to clean up a few loose ends. If you have other outstanding offers, turn them down promptly. Leave them feeling good about you. Don't forget to inform your network about your new position and thank them for their help. You never know when you'll be looking for your next job, so stay well connected.

Take the time to carefully review the materials describing your new corporate benefits. Be sure to take advantage of anything that's relevant. This is especially true of perks that save you money or put additional cash in your pocket, such as retirement plan matching contributions. Develop a plan to manage your finances in a way that puts you on a smooth path to financial independence. Chapter 14 walks you through the details.

The first few months in the new job will be busy and stressful. Get regular exercise, plenty of sleep, and eat well. Keep an eye on your work hours to ensure you're keeping a sustainable pace. Use your honeymoon period to create some early wins at the office. Get to know the people and their roles. Learn to manage upwards, downwards, and sideways. Take a look at Chapter 15 for suggestions on dealing with these and related topics.

The job search process may initially seem overwhelming in complexity and scope. By partitioning and sequencing each component as outlined above, we believe it'll feel manageable and achievable. Complete each step, and then move on to the next when you're ready. A great job is your reward at the end!

CHAPTER 3

YOUR LIFE VISION

*"The only thing worse than being blind
is having sight and no vision."*
– HELEN KELLER

Since you'll spend so many of your waking hours working for an income now and over the next 30 to 40 years, why not find something you'll really love doing? A career that makes you happy, satisfies your intellectual curiosity, and provides sufficient income to support your lifestyle is out there. Your first task is to figure out what it is. For us, a Life Vision has been a valuable tool to help do that.

A Life Vision is a written description of what you'd like your life to look like five or more years in the future. It is an inspiring and compelling narrative that paints a picture of your life when your goals and dreams have been fulfilled and you're living in a way that's consistent with your values. Your Life Vision is written in the present tense, as though it has already unfolded the way you'd like. Think of it as an ongoing inspiration for living your life and for going after your dreams. It will also help focus your actions as you think about making big life plans and decisions.

Career will likely be a significant component of your Life Vision. We also typically see descriptions of relationships, lifestyle, goals, dreams, and big life events. Writing a vision statement requires introspection, soul searching, and inspiration. It's a time to focus on the possible, without the constraints sometimes imposed by everyday life.

Those who have read Jim's book, *From Ramen to Riches: Building Wealth in Your 20s*, will recognize some of the Life Visioning material that follows. If so, we ask that you read this from a perspective of improving on the Life Vision you previously wrote, with a specific focus on career. We believe this topic is so valuable and helpful that it is worth discussing here, even if it risks a repeat for some readers.

What Does a Life Vision Look Like?

We became believers in the visioning process over a decade ago when Lauren was in the midst of a career transition. She had worked a variety of jobs in several industries over the prior 20 years. While each job moved her higher up the corporate ladder, she wasn't feeling like she'd found her true calling. We stepped back and took a look at the big picture. What did we want out of life? How would our work contributions fit into that picture?

After a lot of discussion, we came up with the following vision:

Our Lives Together

"We wake up each morning with the love we feel for each other, our friends, our family, and everyone in our lives. We are the proud parents of a beautiful child who is growing up to be a wonderful human being. We cherish our friends and family and actively include them and their contributions in our lives.

The company we've created is making a powerful difference in the lives of the people we serve by helping them realize their dreams. Our contributions center on empowering people and bringing them joy. We conduct ourselves with integrity, our work feels like play, and everyone we work with loves their job more than anything they've ever done.

Our frequent travels around the world are filled with adventure, fun, and romance. And when we return to San Francisco, we're inspired each day with its energy, diversity, food, and beauty. We're lucky to live here.

At the end of each day as we fall asleep in each other's arms, we're grateful for each other and our child, for our health, and for what we have and what we give. We can't wait for tomorrow!"

We framed the finished product and hung it on a wall where we could easily see it. At the time we wrote it, we were childless and seemed to have little possibility of being parents because Lauren was 44 years old. Well, two years later Lauren gave birth to our now 10-year-old son.

Similarly, we had both been working for corporate paychecks for a couple of decades, and the dream of running our own company had barely occurred to us prior to sitting back and thinking about what we really wanted. Lauren now runs her own consulting company that helps people pursue their dreams and become more successful leaders. Jim has a career as a writer. Finally, this book itself is the direct result of some of the thinking in our vision: "making a powerful difference...by helping people realize their dreams. Our contributions center on empowering people and bringing them joy."

To get started writing your vision, find a place that inspires you, where you can think big about your life. Perhaps at the ocean, a lakefront, or a mountaintop. Pick any place that has significant meaning to you. Allow your mind to dream, to think big. Jot down everything that comes to mind that excites you, that moves you, that inspires you. Don't worry about getting the wording right. You can do that later. Get everything out of your brain and onto the paper. (By the way, if you have a life partner, this is a great exercise to do together. It will help the two of you gain some clarity around how you'd like your life together to unfold.)

As you think about your Life Vision, you can be as specific or vague as you like. It's also perfectly fine to include a specific reference to your career goals if that is relevant for you. For example, you could say something like, "Become sufficiently successful in my field of choice by age 40 to have the flexibility to explore other outlets for contributing my talents and passions to the world."

Here are some things to consider as you're thinking about your vision:

- What are you passionate about?
- What dreams did you have as a kid that you'd love to accomplish if there were no constraints on you?
- What kind of work would make you happy and still provide sufficient income to support your lifestyle?
- How do you want to balance your career goals with your life away from work?
- What are your values?
- How do you like spending your free time?
- What unmet educational goals do you have?
- What do you want out of life in the next several years? If it doesn't strain your brain too much, think even longer term.
- What if you get married? Do you want to have children? Will you or your partner stay at home with them? How will the children's college educations be funded?
- What do you want others to say about your life?
- How would you like to give back to the community and the world?

Visit your special place (or places) until the ideas stop coming. Then, gather the ideas into a coherent document that describes where you want to go with your life in the next 10 years. Write it in present tense, as if it is already here. You'll know you're done when you and everyone you share it with is inspired and excited by what they read. Print it on fancy paper, frame it, and hang it on a wall where you can look at it often. Read it whenever you need inspiration. Feel free to change it as your life circumstances evolve or when new ideas show up for you.

At this point, you have an inspiring document containing a vision with several components. Odds are good that your career aspirations are represented in there somewhere. For example, if you wrote, "*I am the CEO of a $10 million company at age 40,*" that is a very specific career vision. Here are a few additional examples:

- "*I enjoy my work as a computer special effects engineer for a preeminent studio in Hollywood.*"
- "*I am so grateful to work for a healthcare company that allows me to contribute my passion for health and fitness to others.*"
- "*After completing my graduate degree, I am now employed as a researcher. My work interests me every day and gives me a chance to make life better for others.*"

Even if your Life Vision has no direct references to your career, we'd wager that you have many components that indirectly refer to, or have an impact on, what you'd like to do for work. Here are two examples to consider:

1. "*I nurture our kids' development by being a stay-at-home parent until the youngest is in elementary school.*" There are clues to future careers conveyed in that statement. If being a role model to kids is inspiring, is a teaching or coaching career in your future? A child psychologist? What about creating a part-time, income-producing blog about your experiences as a mom or dad? If you had a career prior to becoming a parent, would you want to work part-time from home during your child-rearing years to keep your hands in that line of work? It may well be that your career calling is to be a stay-at-home parent and the vision crystallizes that for you. If so, terrific! A simple statement like "being a stay-at-home parent" can be examined more closely to

determine whether or not there might be any associated career aspirations, during, after, or both. Here's another one:

2. *"We generously contribute back to the community that has given so much to us."* Again, career aspirations may be interconnected with this statement. Does this mean you donate some of your free time? Is your true calling to be employed by a non-profit that serves a population or cause you care about? Or, does this statement mean you've accumulated so much wealth in your high-paying corporate job that you want to contribute some of that money for the benefit of your community?

Carefully scrutinize what you've written in your vision statement. Talk about it with a friend or your partner if you have one. Look at every statement and discuss what you really mean. And since you are currently in job search mode, think about the implications that your future-state vision has for your life in the present. Specifically, what job or career choices can you make now to steer you in the direction of that desired outcome? (After thinking about this, if you are still vague on your career vision, don't worry. We'll give you help in the self-assessment chapter later on.)

Your next step will be to think about how to turn the vision into reality. There's a Japanese proverb that says, "Vision without action is a daydream. Action without vision is a nightmare." Once you have the vision complete, you'll avoid the nightmare part of the proverb. Now, the trick is to keep this work from becoming just a daydream.

Your vision was written to describe what you'd like your life to look like five to ten years into the future. Next, begin to think about a rough timeframe for how you want to organize your goals so that you can see how all the pieces might fit together holistically. A way to start this planning process is to develop a matrix that looks something like this (for a hypothetical 22-year old):

My life goals and dreams	Next 90 days	2 years	5 years	10 years
My relationships			*Get married*	*Have a child*
My work	*Build my network. Find a job!*	*Get promoted*	*Move into management*	*Start a company*
My adventures		*SCUBA in Australia*	*Learn to fly*	
Things I want to learn		*Learn to paint*	*Finish MBA*	
My financial goals	*Start savings plan*	*Emergency fund complete*	*House down payment*	*$100,000 net worth*
Giving back	*Volunteer at non-profit*	*Develop giving plan*		*Help at kid's pre-school*

The items we've placed in the cells above are obviously just examples. If you are a planner like we are and like this approach, you can put a lot more detail into each cell, making sure that everything in your vision gets mapped into it somewhere. Feel free to include multiple items in a cell if necessary. If you are not a planner, at least do an overview framework like the above to give you perspective.

For each item on your Life Vision that you have placed into one of the boxes on this matrix, we encourage you to develop a plan that works backward into the steps required to make it happen. Start with the items that are furthest in the future. As you move toward the present time, your plans will become more detailed and will have better resolution than those that are far away.

The result is a specific set of actions that set you on your way to achieving your goals and dreams. Clearly, it is easier to work through the steps required for goals that are only a year or two into the future than it is for items that are very long term. That's okay, because once or twice a year you can go through the same process to update and refine the items on your list.

If you are not a planner or the idea of a matrix doesn't resonate, fair enough. (We can hear you now: "How can I possibly know that I'll get married in five years?") The point is that you will need to devise some mechanism that works for you to ensure that the vision and your dreams don't just hang on the wall like a piece of art and never become real for you.

CHAPTER 4

CAREER STRATEGY AND GUIDELINES

"I never did a day's work in my life. It was all fun."
- THOMAS EDISON

Think of your Life Vision as the 30,000-foot view of where you'd like to go with your life. In this chapter, we'll take you down to about 10,000 feet. Using your Life Vision as a guide, you will start outlining how you'd like your career to move forward. Below we provide several guidelines for early career strategy. Think of these as guideposts that will help translate the big picture from your vision into an eventual plan of action for defining your career path and locating a job.

Please recognize that the topics we'll outline here are general guidelines that work for most, but perhaps not all. It's impossible to customize advice in a book the way we can when working with an individual client. (Individualized career strategy usually takes at least five hours of one-to-one coaching.) Nevertheless, these eight guidelines will help you craft an early career strategy. Refine it over time as new opportunities and desires emerge.

Guideline #1: Start with a Large Company

Within an industry or across industries, once you have accumulated work experience, it is generally easier to move from a larger company to a smaller company than the reverse. Here's why large company experience is so valued:

- Odds are higher that people will have heard of the larger company's name. Hiring managers tend to be more impressed with resumes containing employment history with the big guys than with the small fry.

- Employers are more likely to think that bigger companies have their act together more than their smaller brethren. This may or may not be true, but they believe it is.
- Companies like to hire from their bigger competitors, thinking the employee may bring some best practices.
- Employers assume that larger companies train their folks better. Again, this may or may not be true, but they still have the perception of decreased hiring risk.
- Hiring managers will have a better idea of what you can do on the job, since they probably know something about the behemoth on your resume. Here's an analogy. If your resume shows you graduated from an Ivy League college, hiring managers have some confidence that your thinking and writing skills are pretty good simply by virtue of having survived an extremely competitive admissions process, and then making it through four years. Similarly, if you have large company experience, employers have a greater degree of comfort that your fundamental job skills are sound. For example, if you've been a financial analyst for a large Wall Street investment bank, you are very likely to be able to analyze a company based on its financial statements. Similarly, if you've been a marketing assistant at a major consumer products company, you will know the various ways to market and advertise a product in print, TV, and online, and are educated on promotional vehicles like coupons.

In suggesting that you consider a "large company first" strategy, we want to be clear that we are not denigrating or downplaying the wonderful role that smaller firms play in our economy. After a few years working for large corporations, Lauren has spent the majority of her career working for smaller companies. If you are clear that you would thrive best in a company with fewer employees, by all means pursue that goal. Just be open to the possibility that a few years with a larger firm early in your career may be of value to you in the long term.

Guideline #2: Decide on a Line or Staff Role

A line role is a job directly connected to what the company does. Usual line roles include: management, sales, marketing, engineering, and manufacturing. A staff role is one that's involved in supporting the business and enabling it to run effectively. Typical staff roles include finance, human resources (HR), information technology (IT), and purchasing.

Both line roles and staff roles can provide fabulous career paths. Neither is necessarily better than the other. The important thing is that you choose which you want consciously, rather than falling into one or the other without thinking about it.

In general, line roles are better stepping-stones to senior management. The closer you are to the mainstream of a business, the more likely you will continue on a path to an eventual executive role. Career advancement and promotions in line roles come predominantly from proving you can grow the business. You may have expertise in a certain area, such as sales, marketing, product management, engineering, or manufacturing. However, your impact is typically measured by company growth in revenue or profitability.

With staff roles, advancement tends to be within the discipline. While there are a few CFOs who have become CEOs, for example, this is the exception rather than a common occurrence. Advancement in staff roles is often aided by additional credentials and schooling in the subject area. Examples include a Certified Public Accountant (CPA) certification for those in an accounting profession or a Chartered Financial Analyst (CFA) designation for investment analysts. With staff roles, excellence and promotions are often tied to mastery of a subject or discipline.

Certain jobs that are traditionally viewed as staff roles may in fact be line roles if that discipline is the focus of the company. So, if you have accounting expertise and work at a firm that provides external auditing services, you would be in a line role if you are providing services to outside clients. Similarly, if you are an IT person working with clients at a company that provides outsourced IT expertise, you are in a line role. So, if your expertise is in an area traditionally viewed as a staff position and you aspire to eventually move into a senior management job, working at a firm that provides services in your discipline is one possible pathway to consider.

Think carefully about your long-term goals. Would you prefer to build expertise in a specific functional area (either line or staff)? Look for clues from your past. Did you love your major courses and hate the electives? Or, were you excited about the opportunity to learn all kinds of things? Self-knowledge is the key here. If you don't know, have informational interviews with folks in each role you are considering. Find out what their day-to-day life is really like. What resonates with you, and what doesn't?

Guideline #3: Determine Whether to Pursue an Individual Contributor or Managerial Path

Proactively choosing an individual contributor path or a managerial path is the next dimension of your career strategy. (The term "individual contributor" refers to employees who do not have supervisory responsibilities.) We'll be clear up front: both choices are noble callings. Neither is better nor worse than the other. We're simply suggesting that you'll benefit from thinking about your future path now so that you can position yourself for where you want to be down the road a few years hence.

Mark Title, a senior biotechnology executive, offers the following thoughts on an individual contributor path as compared with management:

"Much literature suggests that individual contributors can find lasting career success when all three of the following criteria are met: (1) They become 'subject matter experts' in their field, establishing themselves as irreplaceable in the company; (2) They consistently and diligently keep up with new developments in their field to maintain their edge; and (3) Their work over time remains important to their company and their industry. The last item is totally uncontrollable at the individual level. Mergers and acquisitions, for example, often change the company focus away from one's area of expertise, and technological innovations may make your expertise no longer needed.

In contrast, studies show that those developing their skills in managing others find more lasting opportunities to contribute to their companies and greater flexibility in the face of changing company focus and industry shifts."

The choice of a managerial versus individual contributor path will be obvious for some; for others, it may take several years of work experience to decide. Most jobs early in your career won't be in management, but you need to know whether your chosen role leads in your preferred direction. At a minimum, you'll want to choose a position that won't preclude your ability to move to a different type of role later on.

Individual contributor path

Regardless of your chosen career path, you'll likely start in an individual contributor position. You'll find an amazing variety of these roles. Examples include engineer, quality analyst, accountant, marketing associate, public relations assistant, and procurement specialist. We've even seen corporate pilot and librarian positions. Individual contributors typically specialize in a particular area. As they move from entry level to senior contributors they develop deep expertise in their chosen profession.

To get an idea of what an individual contributor position might be like in your chosen field, we recommend conducting several informational interviews with people who do those jobs. (We'll discuss this more in Chapter 9.) During the informational interviews you can get answers to questions like: "What training opportunities does the company offer to keep skills sharp?" "Are there local professional organizations you'd recommend I join?" "What are the benefits and disadvantages of remaining an individual contributor in your area of specialty?" "What does the career path look like for someone who chooses not to move into management?" Answers to questions like these can help define the direction you'd like to take.

Managerial path

You may have had little or no experience in managing people. So how will you know if you'd like it or not? Look for clues from your past. Have you been in leadership positions in clubs or sports? Have you enjoyed those roles? Can you empathize with others while simultaneously motivating them to get things done?

Conduct informational interviews with people in management positions. What did their paths look like? How did they decide to make the move into management and why? Were they certain they wanted a management path early on or did they migrate to that choice over time? What skills did they need to develop before or soon after moving into management? How did they overcome their hesitation (if any) about leaving behind an individual contributor position? If you are still uncertain, try to position yourself in a role where you can get some informal leadership experience. Management is a skill that can be taught if you develop an interest.

Guideline #4: Look for Companies with Defined Career Paths

Companies that care about defining career paths care about developing people. These are great companies to work for early in your career. Once you're inside such a company, you will have an opportunity to learn what a typical career progression looks like in your chosen area of expertise. You'll be able to work with, and be mentored by, people who have been in your shoes. If you perform well, your management and mentors should help guide you through successive levels of relevant positions.

Yes, people often change companies to get a jump in title or pay, but if you can get that without changing companies, you are way ahead. (This assumes, of course, that you like your current employer.) Advancing within a company allows you to learn the new job without learning a new company at the same time, so you enhance your odds of success. It's probable you'll succeed faster without the dual learning curves.

Please don't assume that we are suggesting you should stay with the same company your entire career. Jim worked at a multinational high-tech company for 25 years, but only because the firm's culture was a good fit with his values and he had plenty of opportunities to move around and grow professionally. Lauren worked for a few huge firms early on and moved to smaller companies after she'd gained experience and realized that was the best environment for her. Working at a company with a defined career path is one way to accelerate professional growth in your chosen area. You can probably find other ways to achieve the same goal. If so, great!

Chances are good that at some point you will feel you have learned all you can or moved as high as possible at a particular company. That's fine. As you accumulate more years of work experience, you'll get better clarity on what should come next. Learn as much as you can where you are, do a good job, and when the time comes to move on, do it with grace and professionalism.

Guideline #5: Start with the End in Mind

Use your Life Vision to help you answer the questions that will arise in your career quest. Knowing something about the endpoint will help you make good interim choices as you move towards your goals. For example, you may already know you want to end up in senior management. Perhaps you know you want to always live in the Pacific Northwest (or New England, or wherever). You may be clear that you eventually want to run your own company. Your Life Vision may describe a specific lifestyle or a desire to contribute back to your community. Each of these gives clues to your career strategy.

Use these to your advantage. Pick out as many clues from your Life Vision as you can, and then figure out how to apply them to your career strategy. For example, if you want to stay in the Pacific Northwest long-term, you'd best focus on industries that are well represented in the area. If you want to make a lot of money, you should focus on industries and functions that pay above-average salaries, incentive pay, or offer generous stock options.

The answers to these questions will help steer you in the right direction. But by all means, be sure to take advantage of unforeseen opportunities as they arise. There is a lot of joy in reinventing yourself along the way, career-wise. Take it from Lauren; she's done it seven times!

Guideline #6: Find Out What Makes People Successful in Your Industry or Function

This will be an ongoing discovery throughout your working career. You may be surprised to find that the answers are not always that easy to uncover. Beyond the technical skills required for a particular profession, you'll discover that successful people have a variety of soft skills to help them advance. Examples might include an ability to work well with others, dependability, and commitment to task.

Take advantage of the opportunity to observe and talk to successful people continually throughout your working life. How do they go about their work? What skills do they have and how do they apply them? While you're in job search mode, informational interviews are one of the best ways to do this. You may also be able to find seminars or presentations aimed at people in your chosen field. Once you are employed, find a successful person to mentor you.

You will learn things like whether an advanced degree is considered a plus (or a necessity) in your field. You'll discover the impact that good people skills might have. You'll learn how much people need to travel in certain roles and whether relocation is expected. The answers are not necessarily bad or good. They are opinions. However, these opinions are great reality checks about whether this is the industry or function for you.

Guideline #7: For Those Who Know They Want to Start Their Own Company

Entrepreneurs are the lifeblood of our economy. Perhaps you have a hot idea that needs to be pursued immediately to catch a market wave. You may also be certain that you need to work for yourself and do your own thing. If so, by all means, follow your dreams. Bill Gates dropped out of Harvard to start Microsoft. He certainly did well. Be aware, however, that the odds do not favor young companies. As entrepreneurs ourselves, we can tell you that running your own firm can be immensely satisfying. It's also a lot of work and can take much longer than you think to generate enough profit to support your lifestyle.

Let us propose a more conservative alternative to those who want to go out on their own eventually. We strongly recommend that you learn as much as you can while working for other peoples' companies. Make your mistakes while it's on someone else's dime. You'll discover there's a lot to learn to make an enterprise successful. Gaining these lessons while working for someone else is an easier way to do it. Learning the hard way while the money is coming out of your own pocket is not very fun and can put your venture at risk.

If your career strategy calls for eventually becoming an entrepreneur, develop a plan to gain experience starting and running a business inside someone else's company. Plan to manage the development of a new product or product line, for example. Target a future job that gives you full profit and loss (P&L) responsibility, such as a division general manager. These experiences will help you develop the skills you need to successfully go out on your own.

If you're certain you want to be your own boss and you want to do it now, who are we to discourage you? Check out **www.nolo.com** or other legal education websites to explore options for how to organize your business. For free or low-cost assistance with getting your venture off the ground and helping it grow, check out SCORE (**www.score.org**). SCORE is a non-profit that is dedicated to helping small businesses through their education and mentoring services. SCORE is supported by the Small Business Administration (SBA). Lauren served as a volunteer counselor at SCORE for several years and was very impressed with their services.

Finally, try to find forums for entrepreneurs that may be available in your community. Some universities host events and groups like this. As you proceed, surround yourself with other entrepreneurs and mentors who know the ropes.

Guideline #8: Expectations for Promotions

In her consulting practice, Lauren works with many senior executives. The subject of promotions comes up frequently enough that we feel it's important to mention briefly here. Many employers are frustrated with what they feel are unrealistic expectations on the part of younger workers. While every ambitious employee wants to rapidly climb the corporate ladder, please be aware that promotions may not happen as quickly as you'd like.

If you are on a managerial track and you're a top performer, plan on at least two to three years for your next promotion. For those planning to remain an individual contributor, be thinking in the range of two to four years. Add an additional year or two if you are an average performer. If you're in a highly technical or scientific field, it could be even longer. Generally speaking, larger companies offer more upward mobility simply because they have more seats to fill.

The estimates above are just generalizations. As always, there are exceptions to every rule. If you are particularly talented and motivated, by all means pursue that promotion when you think you're ready, even if it means moving to another company. Just be aware that your employer may not move as quickly as you might like.

Your Turn: Put Your Career Strategy in Writing

Take a moment now to write out a few sentences on your own career strategy, taking into consideration the guidelines and advice above. Make it concise and crisp. Here's an example:

> *"In five years, I will be a manager at a mid-size online marketing firm in New York with a minimum of four direct reports. I'll be working with a mentor who will help me define a path into senior management. I will be getting my MBA at night."*

If you're not ready or able to do this yet, we'll offer more guidance in the next chapter. You can come back to this later.

We also suggest that you write down a rough timeline for at least the next five years, preferably ten. Include major milestones and things you know you want to learn and accomplish. From this, create lists of career strategy questions that you want to ask in your upcoming informational interviews. These questions might include things like, "How useful is an advanced degree in this field?" or "How can I best position myself to get into management?" Keep your written career strategy handy to review and modify over time—not just in your job search, but at least every six months during your career. It's fine if the destination shifts a bit as you learn more about the world of work. Just make these shifts consciously and thoughtfully.

CHAPTER 5

SELF-ASSESSMENT

*"Your work is to discover your work and
then with all your heart to give yourself to it."*
– BUDDHA

So who are you? What are your strengths? What skills and experience do you bring to the world of work? When you can clearly articulate the answers to those questions, you'll be better equipped to identify a satisfying career path. You'll also come across better in interviews than candidates who haven't done this work.

A rigorous self-assessment will help crystallize those things you really like to do, the topics you're passionate about, and the values that are important in your personal and work lives. Rather than just finding any old job, you'll be better positioned to locate something that lights you up. Barbara Wakefield is a former mid-level manager for a major high-tech company. She currently volunteers her time as a career coach working with young professionals. Barbara says,

> "The number one thing I tell people is to find a career that is true to what you love to do. If you have a passion, follow that dream and you will be happy in your career. Of course making money is important, but not as important as your well-being. There is absolutely nothing worse than being middle aged, having another 20 years to work and realizing that you hate what you do. Money is just not that important.
>
> I have too many friends who ended up in high-tech because we live in Silicon Valley, got used to the money, and couldn't get

out due to ongoing financial commitments. In all cases, they were extremely unhappy with their lives.

So, when people are stuck and can't figure out what they want, I have them stop thinking about work/money, clear their minds, and tell me what they loved doing as a kid.

Here's an example: I once promoted a production employee to work as a computer operator. After a few years he became extremely bored. He did not have a degree so getting into the programming field wasn't going to be easy. I had him tell me what he loved doing. He said he enjoyed construction/cabinet making and being a sports coach. We looked around for jobs within the company that enabled him to get out from behind a desk and use his hands more. He ended up being an IT networking technician responsible for pulling cable and maintaining all of the wiring closets. I told him we couldn't help him out with the baseball coaching, and to look into volunteering as a Little League coach—which he did. He ended up being much happier!"

In this chapter, we'll help you assess your **values**, identify your **passions**, profile your **skills**, and summarize your life and work **experience**. When you have an in-depth understanding of these four components, you will have a picture of yourself that answers the following questions:

1. Under what values do I want to live my life?
2. What things do I really care about?
3. What do I love doing?
4. How would I like to spend my work life?
5. What kind of company would I like to work for? What sort of culture and values must that organization exhibit for me to be happy there?

Your job search notebook will come in handy at this point. We recommend having a place to capture your thoughts and reactions to the questions that follow. Your answers will likely not be complete the first time through. Once you start noodling on this stuff, your brain will generate more ideas at completely random moments. Go back and add to your list when this happens so you don't forget these insights.

Values

Values are the deep, enduring beliefs that you hold most closely to your heart. Values guide your ethics and behavior. They are crucial to feeling whole. Conversely, when they are not upheld (by you or others), you feel empty, uncomfortable, or angry. At a minimum, if your values are violated, you will not feel centered, happy with yourself, or your environment. Knowing your key values will be a strong contributor to your future success and happiness. As Mahatma Gandhi so eloquently put it,

> "Your beliefs become your thoughts. Your thoughts become your words. Your words become your actions. Your actions become your habits. Your habits become your values. Your values become your destiny."

The organizations you work for will also have sets of values. The values a company exhibits must be in reasonably good alignment with your own for the job to be a good match. The key to success here is to first have a good understanding of your personal makeup. Then, develop the skills to assess a company in the same way.

For example, nearly every company has a slogan on the wall that says something like, "People are our most valuable asset." That's great—motherhood and apple pie stuff. The trick is to figure out whether management really "walks the talk." If the senior executives are laying off thousands of people while concurrently buying corporate jets to ferry themselves around, you have a pretty good clue that the corporate values they talk about are just baloney. Management with that behavior quickly generates an environment of distrust and cynicism. Why not work at a much better place?

So, step one is to identify the values that are important to you. Pull out your electronic or paper notebook and use the following questions to generate a list of values:

1. What values underlie your life?
2. What are your family's values?
3. What do you believe deeply in?
4. What values, if violated, would make you uncomfortable?
5. What values, if violated, would make you not want to work at a company?
6. What values would attract you to a company?
7. What traits do you most value in your friends?

8. What value disagreements have made you part ways with a friend?
9. If you were to form a non-profit, what would be its values?
10. What values underlie your religion, spirituality, or beliefs?

Please answer the above questions before looking at the list below. Then, include any from the following table that resonate:

Examples of values (and attributes people value)

Abundance	Achievement	Adventure
Autonomy	Beauty	Challenge
Comfort	Community	Creativity
Dignity	Discovery	Diversity
Duty	Empathy	Empowerment
Endurance	Equality	Excitement
Expertise	Family	Forgiveness
Freedom	Friendship	Fun
Generosity	Giving back	Growth
Health	Helping others	Honesty
Humor	Inclusivity	Independence
Industriousness	Integrity	Intimacy
Joy	Kindness	Laughter
Leadership	Learning	Leisure
Love	Loyalty	Meaning
Nurturance	Openness	Patience
Peace	Personal growth	Play
Pleasure	Power	Positivity
Quality	Recognition	Respect
Reverence	Safety	Security
Self-esteem	Self-fulfillment	Serendipity
Spirituality	Spontaneity	Trust
Uniqueness	Volunteering	Wisdom

As you went through the above list, did you find yourself highlighting the majority of them? If so, that's understandable. Most people find these attributes to be positive and compelling. A lengthy list of values is great, but will not be as useful as identifying the critical few that help define who you are. Those will become an important measuring stick for deciding on your next job.

If your values list contains more than 10, we'd recommend sorting it so that the highest priority values stand out clearly. Carefully look through your list and identify those you couldn't live without. Limit that set of highest-priority values to no more than one-third of your list. Assign an "A" to those items. Continue on, assigning a "B" to the next third and a "C" to the bottom third. So, if you have 15 items on the list, you would end up with five each. Your "A" items should be your primary focus. The others are useful, but secondary.

The resulting list will serve you in a couple ways. First, you may find that you get better perspective on the type of work you would enjoy. For example, if your list is weighted heavily with values like community, making a difference, giving back, and helping others, you probably wouldn't be very happy as a Wall Street investment banker. Odds are better that you would favor something in the non-profit world, healthcare, or education.

Second, your values list will come in handy when you assess the work culture of a potential employer. An interview is always a two-way street. You are buying as well as selling. You will have numerous opportunities to ask questions of potential managers and colleagues about how the company treats its people, what it does for the community, and how it behaves in the marketplace. Use your ranked list of values to prepare questions to help you get at some of these more intangible issues that will nonetheless be important to your happiness in the workplace.

Passions

What are you passionate about? In the context of finding a job you love, we are referring to the things you love doing with your time and care deeply about. Focusing your work life around something you care about is a win-win. Wouldn't it be great to be paid for something you want to do anyway?

Bring out your notebook again and use the following questions to help you compile a list of passions:

1. What do you love to do?
2. What do you care deeply about?
3. To what do you contribute money?
4. What would you do if money were no object?
5. What did you want to be and love to do when you were a child?
6. What would you do if you won the lottery?
7. What do you spend time doing on the weekends?
8. What draws you to your friends?

9. What are your hobbies?
10. What can you talk endlessly about?

As you think about this list, consider all aspects of your life: spiritual, academic, how you spend your free time, causes that are important to you, and so on. The idea is to assemble themes that these activities may share. What's in common? Why do you gravitate to these things? What are the parts of your life that get you fired up or make you feel light, joyful, and happy?

You may find that your passions evolve as the years pass. Life experience will open new doors that you may or may not choose to enter. Our suspicion is that many things you will become passionate about in the future are a natural outgrowth of who you are now. Take the time to be introspective about what it is that drives you. That effort will set you on a career and life path that brings you joy all along the way.

Skills

Now we start getting to the talents that are important to you and to a future employer. As this chapter focuses on self-assessment, we're trying to get at the heart of what you like to do, what you are good at, and which of these skills are useful in the workplace.

Skills can be separated into two categories. The first are considered the technical or "hard" skills you need to perform a particular job or task. For example, if you aspire to be a software engineer, you need to know how to program a computer. If you want to be in finance, you need to have good analytical skills. The second skill category is often referred to as your "soft" skills. These include things like your ability to cope with change, ease of interacting with other people, communication skills, ability to persuade, leadership skills, and so on. Soft skills can be applied across a variety of industries or situations. Hard skills typically are more narrowly focused to a particular field or job.

Please take some time now to ponder the skills you possess. To help stimulate your thinking, take a look at the 10 questions that follow. Use them to help compile your skills list. It's fine to have examples outside of work, too. Spend time on each question until your brain runs dry.

1. What are you good at?
2. What do you like to do?
3. What skills do you have that a business would value?
4. What are you most proud of?

5. What comes easily to you that others find difficult?
6. What do you do in your free time?
7. What would you want to do with your time if money were no object?
8. What emotional and soft skills do you have? For example, adaptability to change, dependability, empathy, and so on.
9. How would you describe your work ethic and work style?
10. At what subjects did you excel in school?

Cláudia Schwartz is a Principal at HR Results and also the Director of the HR Leadership Program at the University of California, San Diego. Cláudia suggests that you:

"Find the sweet spot of opportunity where your passions and strengths overlap with emerging market demand. First, look back at your life so far. What passions drive you to perform at your best while feeling most energized and fulfilled? What strengths allow you to create your best results (to get the most 'mileage' for your own 'fuel')?

Next, look forward at the external environment and figure out what trends are evolving in the economy, society, technology, science, politics, legislation, etc. that relate to your passions and strengths. Where is the 'pain' or emerging need in the marketplace, and how can you solve it?"

How do your passions, strengths, and skills intersect with the marketplace trends you see in your areas of interest? Consider the suggestions offered by Cláudia and figure out how they map onto the characteristics and goals you identified in your Life Vision. When you're finished with this exercise, the resulting list will describe what you are good at and enjoy, along with an initial assessment of how these skills correlate to relevant external market trends. These are the things you will want to utilize in a future career. Next, the list will provide valuable input for your resume. Finally, you will find it handy for interview preparation. As you look at your list, pick the top five skills you want to use in your next job. Refining the list in this way can add additional clarity and focus.

Experience

When thinking about finding a job you love, your life and work experiences are key components. In this chapter, we'll focus on experiences that have resonated in a positive way. Later, we'll build on this to summarize your experience from the perspective of a potential employer.

Think about your experience in the context of understanding who you are, what makes you happy, and where you like to spend your time. With your notebook handy, please answer the following questions:

1. Consider any jobs you have held. Several are likely formal assignments that earned an official paycheck. Others may have been internships, or tasks like babysitting, lawn mowing for neighbors, and so on. Create a table that lists each job. Add a column to describe aspects of each job that you liked.

2. Think about memberships in clubs or other extracurricular activities. What were your roles in those organizations? What aspect of those roles made you happy? Add those items to the above.

3. In what sporting or other competitive activities have you participated? Think about when you were successful. When did you feel at your best? What was it about your performance that inspired you? Again, summarize your reactions on the skills list.

4. Finally, jot down your hobbies and other activities where you like to spend your free time. What skills do these activities have in common? Why are you drawn to them? Add to your lists as appropriate.

Take a look at what you've written. What are the key themes? Are there any surprises? What do all these experiences and activities have in common? What drew you to them? Try to summarize into seven to ten bullet points.

Putting It All Together

When you have completed your self-assessment, your notebook will contain a high-level summary of your values, passions, skills, and experiences. Carefully study the lists you created in this chapter. Narrow down to the top five in each area. Create a self-assessment summary table with a column for each and list them on one page. You'll end up with your five top values in column one, five top passions in column two, five top skills in column three, and five top areas of relevant work experience in column four. Here is an example for a client we'll call Lisa:

Values	Passions	Skills	Relevant experience
Honesty	Travel	Initiative	Financial analyst
Accountability	Criminal justice	Organization	Tutor
Integrity	Puzzles	Efficiency	Graded papers
Commitment	Environment	Analytical	Research assistant
Directness	Independence	Mechanical	Tour guide

Compare the self-assessment summary table you just created with the Life Vision you assembled earlier. Do you notice any common themes? Are there any surprises or "Aha!" moments?

You now want to use these values, skills, passions, and experience to map to possible roles and industries. Start on your own and see what roles and industries come to mind when looking at your own summary table like the one above. Then, share your top five lists and your Life Vision with people you know and trust who have experience in the working world. Tell them you are working on discovering jobs that mesh with your vision, values, passions, skills, and experiences. Ask for their perspective, opinions, and specific ideas for possible jobs that fit with you. The result is a list of potential job and industry combinations to explore.

Based on her lists, Lisa came up with the following possibilities after consulting with others:

Industries Lisa is attracted to:

1. Criminal justice
2. Green energy
3. Biotech
4. Travel
5. Technology

Roles she is interesting in exploring:

1. Market researcher
2. Research analyst
3. Court reporter
4. Financial analyst
5. Adventure travel planner

Next, choose one or two roles or industry combinations you want to investigate first. Lisa chose market researcher (in environmental, biotech, or technology companies) and court reporter to explore. Know that you may go back to these roles and industries in the future and choose others if what you explore doesn't turn out to be a fit or if you discover another promising industry. Note, however, that selecting these role and industry possibilities is a crucial part of your search. Take time to be sure you have come up with options that truly appeal to you.

There's one more thing you need to do before diving into research on the jobs and industry combinations you've selected. You'll need a set of criteria against which you'll measure these jobs to see whether they'll be a fit for you. That is the focus of the next chapter.

CHAPTER 6

YOUR JOB CRITERIA

"Pleasure in the job puts perfection in the work."
– ARISTOTLE

Let's review the tools we've assembled so far. You developed a Life Vision that sketched out the big picture of what you want out of life over the next several years. From there, you outlined your career strategy. During the self-assessment process, you figured out your skills and passions and began to map them to specific jobs and industries. You've even gone so far as choosing one or two roles and industry combinations to explore further. Now, let's bring all this work together to create specific job criteria just for you.

You'll create two sets of criteria by the time you finish this chapter. "Ideal job criteria" will be a set of characteristics that describe your dream job. These are the areas where your job quest will be focused and upon which your ultimate decision will be based. You'll also develop "must-have job criteria." These are things that must be there to even consider a job. A potential job missing any elements on this list automatically moves to the do-not-consider pile. By knowing your non-starters in advance, you can rule out opportunities that don't fit before you waste a moment of your time.

Purpose of Ideal Job Criteria

The ideal job criteria you'll develop here will clearly define a prioritized set of requirements for the position you seek. This will assist you in developing questions to ask during informational and formal interviews. It will also help you inform your network of the type of position you're seeking.

Additionally, these ideal job criteria will become the benchmark against which you will rate potential job possibilities and offers. You want to be happy in the job you choose. At some point in your search, you'll be looking at a job offer. A win-win is for you to love your job and be good at it, and for the employer to be delighted with you and the value you bring. How can you do that? Susan Penn, a Vice President of HR, points out the following:

> "Determine not only what you want to do, but where your strengths lie. Figure out what types of environments make you thrive. For example, if you enjoy relating with people and influencing outcomes, be sure to take this into account in your job search. Finding a position that will play to your strengths is the key to happiness and success, in addition to working with people who enjoy and appreciate you. Okay, that and a boatload of money. (Just kidding)."

By specifying your ideal criteria in advance, you will be clear about what you want. You will also be better able to focus your energies during job search and evaluate an employment offer when it comes. After all, it's only going to work out if both sides' needs are met. We're not suggesting that you won't compromise on some things. Even though we'll be talking about "ideal" criteria, no job is perfect. You just want to get as close as you can.

With luck, you'll be in the happy position of considering multiple offers. Yes, this does happen, even in a weak economy. The ideal job criteria you'll develop here will enable you to objectively weigh the pros and cons of each against a pre-defined and prioritized set of requirements.

Possible Job Criteria Choices

The list below contains common criteria job searchers use to evaluate positions. Each one needs to be customized to your particular needs and wants. Some of these will resonate, some won't. At the end of this chapter, you want to end up with a pared-down list of ideal job criteria that really matters to you.

Take out your notebook, and then look at each of the items below. Ignore those you don't care about. If a particular item resonates with you, please take a minute to note it down with a few words or phrases that describe exactly what you want. For example, under "excellent direct boss," you might note: "Does not micro-manage me. Available for help and support when I need it."

Here's the laundry list to help you choose your key criteria. Only choose those that are truly important to you:

- **Excellent direct boss:** One person's great boss might be another's nightmare. How would you describe what you want from a manager? Supportive? Challenging? Effective? Well-networked?
- **Specific role/work:** Clearly define what you want to be doing.
- **Income of $_____:** We'd suggest you write down two numbers here. The first should be your ideal salary. The second should be the minimum amount you need to even consider a particular position. Later in this chapter, you'll see how the second number will become part of your up-front screening criteria.
- **Great product or service:** When you think of a great product or service, what comes to mind? Describe what you mean.
- **Colleagues I enjoy:** Describe further.
- **Excellent training program**
- **Opportunity for advancement**
- **Ability to earn additional income through commission or bonus**
- **Commute of less than ___ minutes (or miles):** Here, too, if it matters to you, you'll want to write down an absolute maximum length you'd accept.
- **Location:** Are you willing to move, or desiring to do so? What is the ideal location for you?
- **Company culture:** What do you want the working environment to be like? It's important that the culture resonates with you. Our colleague Diane, a Vice President of HR, says she once walked into a Silicon Valley interview in a serious suit and was interviewed by a guy in shorts and sandals with his feet up on the desk. The interview lasted 10 minutes. It was not a cultural fit. (It's good they both realized this quickly!) Consider this one carefully, as company culture has a big impact on most people.
- **Company values**
- **Work/life balance:** What does that mean to you?
- **Good future prospects for company/industry**
- **Flexible hours:** Define what that looks like.
- **Team environment:** What does "team" look like for you?
- **Physical work environment:** Are you okay being a cubicle dweller or would that drive you insane? Do you need outside light? Or, are you pretty happy whatever the work environment?

- **Company size:** Define your ideal number of employees or revenues.
- **Ability to work from home:** If so, how often?
- **Travel:** Define the minimum and/or maximum.
- **Ability to work outside or in different company locations:** In other words, you're not stuck at a desk the entire time.
- **Autonomy**
- **Benefits and compensation package as a whole:** If a certain benefit is essential, such as a robust medical plan, call it out.

After you have made your way through our list, add any other items that we have not included that would have a strong influence on your decision.

Review your customized list, with choices from the above and any you've added. Narrow your list to a maximum of five to seven ideal criteria. These should be the ones that would truly affect your decision whether or not to accept a job offer. Be honest with yourself about what really matters.

Prioritization

To show you how to put your ideal job criteria in priority order, let's take a look at the top five unranked criteria for two hypothetical job seekers, who we'll call Matt and Gloria:

Matt's Top 5 ideal criteria	Gloria's Top 5 ideal criteria
Company culture	Role: Salesperson
Role: Admin Assistant	Opportunity for advancement
Team environment	Salary of at least $60,000
Work/life balance	Unlimited commission potential
Commute of less than 20 minutes	Excellent training program

Start by deciding which one of the criteria is most important and which one is the least important. Then place the others in between. If you are looking at a pair of criteria and just can't decide which is more important, ask yourself, "If I could only have one of these criteria, which one would I choose?" That's the one you'd put next on the list.

So, in our example, Matt's prioritization resulted in the following order:

1. Short commute
2. Work/life balance
3. Company culture
4. Team environment
5. Role of administrative assistant

Notice that these results indicate he's pretty flexible about the role he obtains and may be willing to consider others. On the other hand, he really cares about his commute and work/life balance.

Gloria completed her prioritization and ended up with these results:

1. Sales role
2. Unlimited commission
3. Excellent training
4. Salary of at least $60,000
5. Opportunity for advancement

In Gloria's case, it's clear she wants to be in sales with a possibility for large commissions based on her success closing deals. She's confident in her sales skills and wants her compensation to strongly reward excellent results.

Take the time now to prioritize your top ideal job criteria. You'll use the resulting list frequently in the job search process. It'll be especially handy when networking, informational interviewing, preparing for formal interviews, and evaluating job offers.

Must-Have Job Criteria

We'll next ask you to create one more list. This one will contain your must-have job criteria to help you screen out potential positions that contain deal breakers. All the elements on the resulting list must be present for you to even consider applying for a particular job. This way, you avoid wasting your time and the employer's time by applying for a position that won't work out. You'll also stay more focused and keep your momentum going on those jobs that are truly viable opportunities.

Now, rather than thinking about ideal, think about what a job absolutely must have to even consider it. Remember that anything that ends up on this list is an absolute deal breaker. You would not even bother to apply for a job that doesn't meet these essentials. So, be judicious in what you put on the list. Sometimes job seekers only end up with one "must-have," which is commonly a minimum salary number. You will probably have somewhere between one and five criteria.

In the career coaching work Lauren does, here are a few of the must-have items that typically show up for people:

1. **Minimum salary of $_____.** If you are new to the work force, calculating this number can be a bit tricky. Getting paid something is generally better than being unemployed! Do a bottoms-up financial analysis to determine what your absolute minimum salary is, based on your needs (not wants). Do a monthly bare-bones budget, multiply by 12, and then add in the amount of taxes you would need to pay. (Talk to a financial professional or other knowledgeable person if you need help estimating your tax liability.) The resulting number is the absolute minimum you would accept for a full-time job.

2. **Job must be located in a certain city.** If you really want to be based in a certain locale, put it on the list. In our opinion, relocating to a place where you don't want to live is too big a compromise to make for a job. There are enough jobs available almost anywhere for you to be able to find at least one. Be clear about how flexible (or not) you're willing to be. For example, if you grew up in Boston and prefer to stay nearby, are you flexible to work anywhere in New England that is within a few hours' drive? Similarly, if you would consider several places, know that up front and write it down under your "ideal job criteria," since it's not a "must have."

3. **Maximum commute of ___ minutes.** Know what you can handle before it becomes a health issue or serious lifestyle compromise. If public transportation is an option, this time may be longer than if driving, since you can potentially be productive during the commute.

4. **Work-related travel less than (or at least) ___%.** Corporate travel has health and lifestyle implications. Some people love to travel; others despise it. If you have young children, for example, excessive travel for work might be a real problem. Conversely, you may be open to any amount of travel and this wouldn't be a constraint for you.

5. **Product or service must be something I think is good for the world.** If you wouldn't work for companies or industries that aren't in alignment with your environmental, human welfare,

ethical, or other standards, be clear about that in your search and rule out any potential jobs in any firms or industries you don't believe in. Live your values and you'll be happier.

Take the time now to determine and write down your "must haves." You may have none, only one, or several. Double-check yourself by asking, "If a potential job was missing this particular mandatory item, would I turn it down, regardless of all other positive factors?" If the answer is truly yes, then that criterion belongs on your "must-have" list. Don't apply to any job that has gaps in these essential requirements.

Next Steps for Your Job Criteria

Show your job criteria lists to a few friends and family members. Ask them if the criteria sound like you. It's always a good idea to validate your work.

As you proceed in your job search, use the "must-have" list to decide whether to even apply for a particular position. The ideal criteria will help you ask good questions during interviews. They will also help you assess how each potential job maps to your ideal. We'll refer to your prioritized ideal job criteria again in Chapter 13, "Negotiating and Choosing." You'll see then how they can help you with your employment decision, especially if you're looking at multiple job offers.

Keep these lists accessible as you continue through your job search. They will keep you focused on the important things you want to find in a job. You have created your "North Star" to guide you forward in your search.

CHAPTER 7

YOUR RESUME

"Our work is the presentation of our capabilities."
– EDWARD GIBBON

Your resume is the presentation of yourself to the world of work. If done well, it may open doors to a future employer. You will not get a job based only on your paper or electronic resume. However, a well-constructed document is virtually a necessity to pass the first screening test.

Your resume is a crisp and clear description of who you are and what you bring to a potential employer. It summarizes the following:

- **Job objective**: A one or two-sentence description that clearly specifies what type of job you want.
- **Experience**: Your work and other experiences that demonstrate useful accomplishments and results.
- **Skills**: While not necessarily a separate section, you want to make sure your resume highlights your key skills and desirable workplace traits.
- **Education and training:** Your college education, including major course of study and other relevant training.
- **Interesting tidbits:** A small amount of other information or description of personal traits that makes a resume screener want to meet you!

Your goal is to crisply summarize everything a screener needs to know so that you stand out as a viable candidate. Even though you may spend hours crafting something that looks polished and professional, a busy screener will be finished with it faster than a kid attacking a chocolate chip cookie. Here are the brutal facts:

- If you submit your resume online in response to a job posting, the first screen is likely to be done by a computer algorithm. This is especially true at larger companies that receive thousands of resumes. You will be chosen for the next phase only if you have the requisite educational degree, years of experience, and relevant keywords to help the software locate potential matches.
- Most human screeners will spend only 30 to 60 seconds looking at a resume, deciding if you are "in," "out," or "maybe."
- If someone known to the hiring manager or recruiter has introduced you to the company, your chances of at least a phone screen are far higher than someone who has blindly submitted an application.

The screening process at companies is similar to a college admissions procedure. Once your resume lands in the overflowing email inbox of a recruiter, it's one of potentially hundreds for a single job opening. The recruiter is also likely screening for multiple open positions. Like college admissions, many of your competitors look great on paper. The recruiter has limited time and resources to select a much smaller number of candidates for a phone screen or interview. Your goal is to maximize the probability that your resume moves to the "in" group.

If you have no other connection to the company, the best you can do is not flub the introduction that your resume makes for you. (This is one reason why we strongly recommend getting networked into a company by someone you know, rather than relying on an online application. More on that in Chapter 8.) Even if you are lucky enough to have a contact inside the hiring firm, your resume has to be good enough to convince a hiring manager that it's worth the time to move to the next step.

Resume "Do's and Don'ts"

Resumes can be presented in a variety of styles and formats. However, a few key rules apply all the time. Here are the basics:

- Keep it to one page unless you have many years of work experience. After you've been working for more than a decade, two pages is the limit.
- Focus on results and accomplishments, quantifying them whenever possible.
- Think about what makes you different from someone else. What is impressive about YOU? Everyone brings something unique to an organization. Be sure your resume conveys those attributes, skills, and accomplishments.
- Tell the truth! Don't lie about anything.
- Format professionally.
- Write out any uncommon abbreviations the first time.
- Avoid taking full credit for something you did with a team. Instead, explain your role and the results that the team achieved together.
- Highlight your strengths, but don't be braggadocious.
- Sentence fragments are okay on a resume and are often preferred. Remember, crispness and clarity count. Most phrases start with a verb and omit the subject pronoun, since it's all about you.
- Any misspellings or poor grammar will likely earn your beautiful document a quick one-way ticket to the corporate recycle bin. At a minimum, boo-boos like that will raise a red flag about your attention to detail. Kim Box, a former Vice President at Hewlett-Packard, says that, "The worst is typos—a total job opportunity killer. To create a resume without using spell check shows the hiring manager that you don't care enough to take the extra time to do a good job on your resume. If that's the case, why bother hiring you?" Spell check and have several friends review it carefully.
- Make sure the text is filled with relevant keywords for the job you are seeking. This will greatly improve the odds that the corporate matchmaking software selects you.

Action Verbs

Ensure that your resume sparkles with energy. Use action verbs to highlight your skills and experience and convey that you are capable, competent, and committed to results—just what an employer wants! Pretend you are a hiring manager looking at two resumes that are describing exactly the same thing. Which of the following examples get your attention?

1. "Worked on a project to improve the payback period for a new manufacturing process."
2. "Accelerated new manufacturing process payback period by redesigning the work flow."

See how much more powerful the accomplishment sounds in example #2? Action verbs like "accelerated" and "redesigning" grab the reader's attention and emphasize the results. Example #1 is passive and uninteresting, even though the work done was identical. (By the way, both of these examples suffer from lack of specific, measurable results. We'll discuss this later.)

Keywords

Recruiting software looks for keywords in your resume to determine the relevance of your skills and experience to a particular job opening. If the first stop for your resume is the corporate matchmaking software, you can be guaranteed that the computer will be looking for these. There are four types of keywords you'll want to include in your resume: (1) **industry**; (2) **functional**; (2) **job-specific** or **technical**; and (4) **other skills, competencies, and traits**.

Industry keywords indicate the type of business where you worked. Examples include insurance, semi-conductor manufacturing, and investment banking. If the name of a former employer doesn't have the industry name in it, then be sure the description you provide contains it somewhere. A computer may be searching for "insurance" experience, and doesn't know that "ABC Services" means you have it.

Functional keywords refer to the department, operation, or process area within an organization that manages a particular part of the business. Common functional names include human resources, marketing, sales, research and development, manufacturing, finance, and production. These names typically appear at the top of a department's organization chart. Wherever you have worked, if your title doesn't indicate the department/function, make sure to include it in your description of the job.

Job-specific or **technical** keywords are perhaps the most important. These terms describe the work done by a particular job title and the skills and experience required to succeed in such a role. Mechanical engineers, for example, must understand Computer-Aided Design (or CAD). They must also have experience with common CAD software. A resume for someone looking to be hired as a mechanical engineer would therefore need to call out both the specific experience and the name of the actual software that the engineer knows how to use.

Even in less technical jobs you'll want to include job-specific keywords. For example, if you are applying for a human resources position, your resume should include terms like "benefits" or "benefits administration," "recruiting," "screening," and "interviewing." Every job has its key terms. Browse several job descriptions for the specific position (or positions) in which you have an interest. Monster.com would be a good place to go for this. You can also find plenty of sites that offer detailed suggestions for resume keywords by simply Googling the topic.

Finally, your resume should include other keywords that further illustrate your **competencies, other skills,** and **personal traits**. Professional certifications and memberships in recognized industry associations are good examples. So, an accountant would want to list "CPA" or "Certified Public Accountant," together with any related membership in professional organizations.

Personal traits that can be mentioned include many of the soft skills that employers find desirable. Public speaking skills, perseverance, dependability, leadership, teamwork, and other relevant traits are definitely things a potential employer cares about. Capture those areas that are strengths, but don't laundry list them. You need to be believable, descriptive, and very clear about what you are exceptional at. It's even better if these terms emerge in the description of something you accomplished.

Your resume needs to include keywords from all these categories. At the same time, don't make your resume read like it was written for a computer matchmaking algorithm. The keywords help the computer do the first sort, but eventually a real person is going to read it.

Organizing Resume Content

It's finally time to assemble the pieces. To help with this, we'll use an example. The resume shown in Figure 1 is a reproduction of someone's actual resume. To ensure confidentiality, we've changed any information that might identify the particular individual or company. It's not a bad resume, but we'll use it to highlight opportunities to strengthen it.

Figure 1: Sample "Before" Resume

JOHN DOE
123 Main Street, East Overshoe, CA 91234
585-123-4567 | john.doe@awcu.edu

EDUCATION

A West Coast University, Graduate School of Business *Los Angeles, CA*
MBA, Finance, June 2012: **GPA: 3.75**
  - Activities: Finance Club

A West Coast University *Los Angeles, CA*
Bachelor of Arts in Business Administration, June 2011: *GPA: 3.5*
  - Awards: Alpha Beta Chi Scholarship Award (2009-2010)
  - Activities: Member of Alpha Beta Chi Fraternity, Member of College Republicans

A West Coast University *Berlin, Germany*
Study Abroad Program September 2008-April 2009
  - Studied language, history, art, literature and culture for two terms
  - Expanded cultural knowledge and experience through extensive travel in Europe

EXPERIENCE

Really Advanced Biotechnologies, Inc. *San Francisco, CA*
Finance Intern *June 2011 - August 2011*
  - Responsible for tracking marketing expenses throughout the organization by channel and product
  - Proposed changes to Cost Center roll-up structure to regional leaders in Asia so that marketing expenses could be more efficiently analyzed and tracked
  - Developed an employee spending report for a platform leader to analyze company credit card expenses
  - Tracked discrepancies between marketing expense data in SAP and E1 ERP systems

Dos Hermanos Wine Stores, Inc. *Los Angeles, CA*
Brand Ambassador *April 2011 - Present*
  - Performed in-store demos 6-9 hours per week
  - Responsible for raising brand awareness and in-store sales for multiple products through customer interaction and selling techniques
  - Explained features and benefits of various wine and spirit products to convince customers to purchase

ABC Construction, Inc. *San Francisco, CA*
Accounts Payable Manager *May 2011 - August 2010*
- Responsible for managing billing, payment, and coordination with clients
- Reconciled the company accounting system with the bank statements at the end of each month
- Developed an investment memo for future development site in Nevada

XYZ Realty *East Overshoe, CA*
Administrative Assistant *May 2009 - August 2009*
- Performed administrative duties around the office and assisted agents and customers
- Initiated contact with walk-in customers and guided them to agents
- Created presentation booklets for customers and updated listings on company website
- Retained on an as-needed basis during the school year

SKILLS

- Conversational in German
- Proficient in QuickBooks, Microsoft PowerPoint, Excel, and Word
- Experience with ERP systems such as SAP, E1, and EDW

Let's work through each section in turn. Here is the header section of the sample resume:

JOHN DOE
123 Main Street, East Overshoe, CA 91234
585-123-4567 | john.doe@awcu.edu

Your name and contact information goes first. Believe it or not, we have seen resumes with a name but no contact info! Center your name in capital letters on the first line and use a bold typeface. Physical address, phone number, and email get listed just below.

Be sure to list a permanent email address. Your university may allow you to keep a school email address for a period of time, but you can't always count on that being available indefinitely. Given that your resume may surface somewhere months (or even years) later, it's a good idea to be sure that a message from a potential employer doesn't bounce back as undeliverable.

Also, make sure your chosen email name sounds professional. Rhonda Rhyne, a former CEO, reports that she "did not hire a person who had an unprofessional email address on the resume, something along the lines of hotbabe@xxxxx.com." That format might be fine for someone seeking a job in the adult film industry, but it won't work for anyone else.

So, the main thing we would change in the sample resume would be replacing the university email address with something more permanent. You may also want to consider putting the contact information at the margins, so your name stands out even more. Here's how it looks with these changes:

JOHN DOE

123 Main Street
East Overshoe, CA 91234

585-123-4567
john.doe@gmail.com

The **Job Objective** section typically comes next. Your task is to describe in one sentence the position you're after. Be specific about what you want. Ironically, a vague or very general objective statement makes it less likely that someone will act on your resume. Consider the following two examples:

1. "To find a position where I can use my skills in finance."
2. "Seeking a cost accounting position where I can contribute my expertise in manufacturing production costing."

Put yourself in the shoes of a hiring manager who is reviewing dozens of resumes. Let's say the open position is for a corporate treasury position. Will either of these people land an interview? Unlikely. Here's why: The hiring manager is looking for someone interested in corporate treasury. The ideal candidate will not only be passionate about that work, but will also have experience in that area. Person #1's job objective conveys neither. Person #2 is also not a good fit because his interest lies in cost accounting. It's clear that this candidate is specifically looking for a cost accounting role. Even if this job isn't a good fit, the hiring manager might have a colleague with an opening for a manufacturing cost accountant. Which resume do you think will be forwarded?

Consider the same example. However, this time the hiring manager works in cost accounting. Which resume will more likely move to the "in" pile? You got it. Person #2 is passionate about cost accounting. (Yes, some people really are passionate about cost accounting, believe it or not.) It's also clear that he or she has relevant experience in this area. The hiring manager is much more likely to continue on to the next section of the resume. Person #1 is out of luck in both examples. If your objective elicits the question, "What do you really want to do?" it's not specific enough.

The Job Objective is also a great way to highlight some of your job-specific skills and character traits. Take a look at a few sample job objectives:

1. "To contribute my sales skills, gregarious nature, love of technology, and competitiveness to growing revenues for a high-tech company."
2. "To improve the effectiveness of a marketing department by using my event planning experience, communication skills, and strong attention to detail."

Notice that these sound like real people, not "cookie cutters."

Okay, time to return to our example resume. In this case, it is missing the Job Objective section completely. In our opinion, this is a significant gap in what needs to be communicated to a potential employer. Again, the more specific you can be about what you want, the greater the likelihood that you'll get it. (Note that it is okay to change the objective if you are applying to a couple of different types of jobs.) So, we'll revise the resume to add an objective, as follows:

JOB OBJECTIVE

To grow the revenues of a nutrition company by contributing my sales skills, competitiveness, ease with people, and integrity.

Your next decision is whether to put the **Experience** or **Education** section after the Job Objective. People who have been working for several years typically list their relevant work experience first. Education eventually becomes secondary. However, if you are relatively new to the workforce, you could consider describing your education ahead of experience. Our advice would be to start with whichever section makes you look the best.

Because John Doe has just received his degree, we'll put his education section first. The **Education** component of your resume should include the name of the college or university, degree obtained, concentration/major, and year of graduation. Be sure to include any academic honors you received, relevant club memberships (especially if you had a leadership role), and anything else that helps you stand out from the crowd. If you worked during school to finance at least 25% of your education, put that in too. Mention your GPA if it is good (above 3.3 or so). Otherwise leave it off. Again, focus on highlighting the good stuff.

High school education details are generally left out, with a few exceptions. You may want to include this if: (a) you have little or no work experience; (b) you attended a prestigious secondary institution; (c) you would like to highlight some particularly impressive honors, accomplishments, or activities; or (d) you have not attended college. Once you're over age 22, your high school days are over for good, especially on a resume.

We worked with this job seeker to highlight a few things he missed, and to delete a few things in favor of more powerful points. Notice, for example, that we deleted the "Member of College Republicans" statement. What if the person reviewing your resume is an avid Democrat who thinks that the Republican Party is the worst thing to ever happen to this country (or vice versa)? As a general rule, we suggest keeping topics like religion and politics out of work. Of course, if you intend to work for a religious or political organization, that's different. If this person had been in a leadership role in the College Republicans organization, we'd probably advise keeping it because it showcases a skill useful to work.

Here's how the sample resume Education section looks after we've changed it to reflect these suggestions:

EDUCATION

A West Coast University, Graduate School of Business   *Los Angeles, CA*
MBA, Finance: **GPA: 3.75**   *June 2012*
- One of only 25 students accepted to renowned 5-year BA/MBA program
- Worked during MBA program, financing 25% of my graduate education

A West Coast University   *Los Angeles, CA*
Bachelor of Arts in Business Administration: *GPA: 3.5*   *June 2011*
- **Awards**: Alpha Beta Chi Scholarship Awards for 3.9 GPA in two terms

A West Coast University   *Berlin, Germany*
Study Abroad Program   *September 2008 - April 2009*
- Studied German language, history, art, and literature
- Expanded cultural knowledge through extensive travel in Europe

The **Experience** section is your opportunity to highlight any work or other relevant experience that a potential employer may find applicable to the job in question. Remember that the recruiter is looking to reduce the risk of hiring. Your resume needs to convey what you have done and what you can do. Realize that the hiring manager is thinking something like, "What can I be sure this person can accomplish when sitting down at his or her desk for the first time?"

Luckily, you've already compiled a list of your work-related experience in Chapter 5. List your most recent work experience first. Show the company name and location, your job title, and dates employed. Emphasize (via formatting) whichever is more important or impressive: company name or job title. Summarize your role and responsibilities in one or two sentences. Immediately following, include three to five bullet points that highlight your accomplishments. These should be results-oriented, specific, and measurable. Avoid boilerplate language. You want to show a hiring manager what you achieved and how you did it.

Use action-verb keywords liberally here. Don't sound passive. Where appropriate, these verbs can highlight your communication skills, teamwork, organization skills, dependability, and the other soft skills that an employer wants to see. Your resume can be a great place, if integrated tactfully, to mention a couple of your inherent, natural traits that you will bring to the job. Figure 2 highlights some of the common traits desired by employers. Be sure not to include overly subjective ones, such as "friendly," or "easy going." Also don't include "humble" or "modest" because saying so makes you neither! If you Google the phrase "resume keyword" as a search topic you'll find many other possibilities.

Carefully review lists like these to find a couple of traits you naturally and consistently exhibit. Highlight these where appropriate on your resume. Be careful to avoid selling yourself as having a trait or skill you don't have. You could end up miserable with a job doing things you don't like or aren't good at. You and your employer will both be unhappy.

Figure 2: Some Traits that Employers Desire

Accountability	Accuracy
Attention to detail	Big picture thinking
Communication	Determination
Energy	Enthusiasm
Follows directions	Hardworking
Honesty	Integrity
Leadership	People skills
Perseverance	Resilience
Public speaking	Sense of humor

Similarly, be sure to include the technical or job-specific keywords that are relevant. You need to keep the computer happy, too. List as many as you can while keeping the document readable. The same advice applies to the job title. For example, if your job title is listed as "Intern – Level 1," the computer will shrug its electronic shoulders. So, in this same example, it would be okay to list your job title as something like "Finance Intern" (if indeed that is what you really were).

One of the benefits of getting older is that you will gain lots of great work experience to add to your resume. In the meantime, don't worry. Even if you are in your early 20s, you likely have many experiences that are appropriate for your resume. Think about things like how you financed your education, internships, jobs you had in high school or summers, and other experiences that demonstrate your ability to get something done.

Here's a great example of how one of Lauren's young career coaching clients approached this. He had limited work experience, so he described work he did for his fraternity, as follows:

"Recruited new members into my fraternity and was one of the house managers for a year. Had to motivate the men every day to be active and participate without the ability to pay or give them anything."

He has highlighted several skills that would be of interest to an employer—leadership, motivational skills, sales (recruiting), and teamwork, to name a few. Look at your experiences in this way and call them out.

If your work experience is thin, then put the Education section first, and mention anything in your academic background that an employer might care about. Club activities, leadership roles on big projects, and research work can all be relevant. You have many unique things to share with the working world. Figure out how to identify and highlight those experiences for someone who is hiring.

So, given the above suggestions, let's compare the before and after versions of the sample resume experience section:

Experience Section, Before Edits

EXPERIENCE	
Really Advanced Biotechnologies, Inc.	*San Francisco, CA*
Finance Intern	June 2011 - August 2011

- Responsible for tracking marketing expenses throughout the organization by channel and product
- Proposed changes to Cost Center roll-up structure to regional leaders in Asia so that marketing expenses could be more efficiently analyzed and tracked
- Developed an employee spending report for a platform leader to analyze company credit card expenses
- Tracked discrepancies between marketing expense data in SAP and E1 ERP systems

Dos Hermanos Wine Stores, Inc. *Los Angeles, CA*
Brand Ambassador *April 2011 - Present*
- Performed in-store demos 6-9 hours per week
- Responsible for raising brand awareness and in-store sales for multiple products through customer interaction and selling techniques
- Explained features and benefits of various wine and spirit products to convince customers to purchase

ABC Construction, Inc. *San Francisco, CA*
Accounts Payable Manager *May 2010 - August 2010*
- Responsible for managing billing, payment, and coordination with clients
- Reconciled the company accounting system with the bank statements at the end of each month
- Developed an investment memo for future development site in Nevada

XYZ Realty *East Overshoe, CA*
Administrative Assistant *May 2009 - August 2009*
- Performed administrative duties around the office and assisted agents and customers
- Initiated contact with walk-in customers and guided them to agents
- Created presentation booklets for customers and updated listings on company website
- Retained on an as-needed basis during the school year

Experience Section, After Edits

EXPERIENCE

Really Advanced Biotechnologies, Inc. *San Francisco, CA*
Finance Intern *June 2011 - August 2011*
Responsible for tracking marketing expenses throughout the organization by channel and product. Utilized both SAP and E1 ERP systems.

- Proposed changes to Asian Cost Center roll-up structure, received management approval, and achieved $100,000 in savings through more efficient analysis and tracking.
- Developed an employee spending report to analyze company credit card expenses and target areas for further review.

Dos Hermanos Wine Stores, Inc.   *Los Angeles, CA*
Brand Ambassador   *April 2011 - Present*

While in MBA program, performed in-store demos 6 to 9 hours per week. Quickly learned features of various wine and spirit products, explained them to customers, answered questions, and convinced them to purchase.

- Garnered in-store sales up to $6,500 in a single day. Averaged $1250/day.

ABC Construction, Inc.   *San Francisco, CA*
Accounts Payable Manager   *May 2010 - August 2010*

Managed billing, payment, and client relations for over 180 clients. Entrusted to reconcile the company accounting system with bank statements monthly.

- Developed a proposal for future $1.5M development site in Nevada; project was approved.

XYZ Realty   *East Overshoe, CA*
Administrative Assistant   *May 2009 - August 2009*

Assisted all 14 real estate agents with proposals, contracts, and other mission-critical duties. Initiated contact with all walk-in customers and guided them to agents.

- Created over 200 different presentation booklets for customers.
- Updated numerous real estate listings daily on company website.
- Based on performance, retained on an as-needed basis during the school year.

Notice the key changes. First, several of the bullet points are now quantified and results-oriented. Notice how many more numbers are in the second version. Next, responsibilities and duties are covered in a descriptive paragraph, so that bullet-point results show up that much more. Finally, we added some context, pointing out that the work was done while in the MBA program, which made the number of hours worked much more impressive.

Skills

If it's relevant to the job for which you are applying, you may want to have a section that outlines other skills that haven't yet been called out. Experience with office software and computers is commonly mentioned here. For example, "Proficient in MS-Word and PowerPoint; Extensive experience on both PC and Mac." Mention any expertise with language skills other than English, and to what degree. For example, "Proficient in Spanish, conversational German, can read French."

Personal Interests

Here's where you get to have some fun. What things are really important to who you are? Long-lasting interests, particularly notable experiences, or impressive accomplishments show up here. Let's look at some examples:

- "Have traveled extensively in Europe, Asia, and Africa"
- "Soprano in school choir since age five"
- "Ran my first marathon last year in 2:55"
- "Bicycled from Florida to Maine last summer"

If you have one or two items that you're especially proud of or that highlight your uniqueness, consider including them here. Do remember, though, that this is a professional document. Steer clear of controversial topics or things that aren't appropriate in a work environment.

One final piece of advice: Though you may have a specific job opening in mind when you assemble your resume, be careful to avoid customizing it exactly to that particular job. Yes, you want to show that you have the skills and experience that an employer wants. On the other hand, hiring managers will see through a regurgitation of their own job description. A colleague in a management role at a large high-tech company told us he once received a resume that was practically a photocopy of the job description he had posted. While the candidate was hoping for a positive reception to such a great match in skills and experience, he actually got the opposite.

Cover Letters

The best place to customize your application for a job is in a cover letter or email. This letter is a preface that gives your resume context and relevance. It also allows you to highlight some especially salient points for this particular opportunity. Think of the cover letter as a brief introduction that describes who you are, what you're looking for, and what you bring to the party. We recommend that you always include it with a job application unless they expressly request that you do not submit one.

What you don't want to do is simply echo the ad or job description and state that you have all those characteristics. The cover letter needs to show some original thought, why you care about this company and job, and what makes you an especially good fit over and above what your resume says. This is a good place to give a slightly longer version of one of the bullet point examples in your resume.

You can distinguish yourself from the multitude of other applicants by doing the following in your cover letter or email:

- Find out the name of the person who is doing the hiring and address the cover letter directly to him or her. Using the hiring manager's name is best if you can find it. At a minimum, you should be able to find the name of the head of HR. Use it.
- If you have been able to find a connection into the company, use that person's name in the first or second sentence of the cover letter. Explain WHY they referred you.
- State a compelling reason why you want to work in that company or role.
- Craft a well-written, thoughtful, concise, and grammatically correct letter.
- Highlight any particularly relevant characteristics, traits, or experiences.
- Use a closing phrase other than "Sincerely." "Respectfully yours" is nice, but only if you can say it with a straight face. "Awaiting your call" sounds a bit desperate, but "Looking forward to hearing from you" could work. Make it uniquely you.

Here's what a cover letter might look like for our friend John Doe, of sample resume fame:

Sample Cover Letter for John Doe

123 Main Street
East Overshoe, California

October 1, 2012

Ms. June Bountiful
ABC Nutrition Company
123 Avocado Street
Palmfrond, AZ 90000

Dear Ms. Bountiful,

Elsie Aimes, who speaks very highly of ABC Nutrition, suggested that I contact you about employment opportunities. Elsie and I worked together at Dos Hermanos Wine Stores. Because she knows my sales performance, she felt that you might be able to use my skills to help your strongly performing company grow even faster.

ABC Nutrition has been on my radar for a while, due to your reputation for having a culture that has spurred ABC to compete effectively while creating a great place to work. I also appreciate the many contributions your company has made to the community.

My passion for health, sports, and nutrition means that I am very interested in contributing to your company. Attached is my resume giving more details of my experience. Feel free to call Elsie if you would like additional input from her as well.

I look forward to hearing from you soon.

Respectfully yours,
John Doe

585-123-4567
john-doe@gmail.com

Standing Out from the Crowd

Sometimes it doesn't hurt to use a bit of creativity to grab a potential employer's attention. Susan Penn, a Vice President of HR, told us she "once received a resume with a pair of sandals glued to the outside of the envelope, with a note that said, 'I'd walk a mile in flip flops for a job with your company.' We hired her." You could consider trying something unusual when you send in your resume and cover letter if it fits who you are and isn't overtly goofy, cutesy, or unprofessional. Falling into the latter category is another resume Susan received with the woman's full body picture and measurements. That one went right to the recycle bin.

Here's another great tip from Cláudia Schwartz. She is the Founder of HR Results, a human resources consulting firm, and the Director of the HR Leadership Program at the University of California, San Diego:

"A practical tip that most candidates are not yet using is to create a QR code that leads to your LinkedIn® profile, resume, and/or personal website that showcases samples of your work achievements. Have your QR code readily accessible in your smart phone, so you can show it to anyone you talk to anywhere, from networking events to the line at a fast food restaurant. Using the QR reader app on their phone, those you talk to can have instant access to what they need to help you find a job. As an HR professional, I have instantly pulled information on people I just met at the most unforeseen places. If what they had to offer matched an opportunity with a company I knew, I talked to them on the spot about next steps."

If you are not familiar with QR codes, these are the funny-looking boxes with black and white squares inside that you may have seen in some printed advertisements. They are conceptually similar to the old-fashioned bar code and have started appearing everywhere. When you start networking, your custom QR code will be a very handy tool to use in your job search.

Making It Happen

Once you've put your resume and sample cover letters together, set them aside for a couple days. Then come back and look at them. Do they accurately describe you? Do you look at the resume and cover letter and feel proud? If not, keep working on them until you do. Show both documents to several people and get feedback. Be prepared to revise them several times until you have editions of both that shine. Remember that your goals are:

1. To powerfully represent who you are;
2. To get the resume past the corporate matchmaking software;
3. To stand out to a human reviewer.

The last preparatory steps in the job search process are completing your resume and cover letter. Now it's time to go out into the world to let people know what you're looking for and to discover job openings that are a good fit with your skills and interests.

CHAPTER 8

IT'S ALL ABOUT YOUR NETWORK

"Keep away from people who try to belittle your ambitions.
Small people always do that, but the really great
make you feel that you, too, can become great."
– MARK TWAIN

Have you heard the saying, "It's not what you know, it's who you know?" While the expression is perhaps a bit cynical, there's an element of truth to it. Put yourself in the shoes of a hiring manager looking at a stack of 100 resumes belonging to people the manager has never met. While many look good on paper, it takes a lot of due diligence to figure out if the person described in the resume is really as fabulous as the document indicates.

Let's assume, then, that the hiring manager heads out to lunch with a friend and says, "I have an engineering opening in my R&D lab. Do you know anyone who might be a good fit?" The friend replies, "I don't, but my wife just met the most amazing recent graduate who really impressed her. You should ask her." Which person is more likely to get a follow-up call from the hiring manager: someone from the stack of 100 resumes or the person who came in as a referral from a trusted source?

About 70 to 90% of jobs are secured through networking. You should spend job search time proportionally to this statistic. That is, you should be spending 70 to 90% of your efforts cultivating your network. This is the most likely way you will connect with someone who has an open position.

One of our favorite stories on the value of networking comes from Susan Penn, a Vice President of HR. Susan said,

"One of the best lessons I learned while networking was learning to do the opposite of what common theory was at that time. Rather than rehearse a networking speech, I researched the person I was going to meet, and then dropped expectations in regards to outcome. I found that I thoroughly enjoyed the networking experience, as I simply wanted to get to know people in the industry I was pursuing. I built relationships that are still important to me, and made a few really good friends in the process. I know I could reach out to these people again, as they could to me.

My current position occurred due to networking. I wanted to meet a contractor who had provided an interesting talk at a meeting I attended. We met for lunch, shared stories about leadership training and development, and his current contracting organization came up. He told me they were looking for an HR professional. However, he knew the position was not at my level. I offered to help them with the search. After all, I knew several qualified people who were out in the market, and I could help the company as well as an HR colleague. The organization decided to elevate the position, and the rest is history."

Our own experience is similar. Jim found his first job by luck (unsolicited submission of a resume). Every job that followed resulted from his network. In her career, Lauren has changed industries several times as a senior executive. In the process she built a very broad professional network that has helped her find new jobs and, more recently, consulting clients.

When you're new to the workforce, your network will not be as robust as it will be after you've accumulated several years' experience. Don't let this discourage you. Here's the key to success:

It's who you can <u>get</u> to know.
(Not necessarily who you know right now.)

What's a Network and Who's in It?

For the purpose of job search, your potential network is the set of people you know combined with the set of people they know, and the set of people they in turn know. Sometimes one of these second or third level connections ("a friend of a friend of a friend") may be your ticket to the dream job interview.

If you think of your network as a dartboard with several concentric circles, the center ring contains the people you know well. The people in the outer rings are those you do not know as well, yet can still play an important role in your job search. In building your network, your goal is to meet people in each of those dartboard rings who will lead you toward potential jobs.

Don't despair if you're feeling like your network isn't very substantial. You already know more people than you might think. Take out a piece of paper or your electronic notebook and jot down everyone you know. (Seriously, do this!) The obvious ones would include your friends, your friends' parents, your parents' friends, and professors.

What about the less obvious ones? Hair stylist? Fitness trainer? High school teachers? Relatives? Coffee shop barista? You never know who they know. Try hanging out in a coffee shop that's located in a complex with corporate office buildings. How many managers do you think stop in for a customized jolt of caffeine without even having to give their order? After you do this exercise, you might be surprised by how long the list gets.

How to Build Your Network

Targeting individuals to add to your network takes thought and effort. If you're an introvert, this might be uncomfortable at times. However, since your goal is to find a great job, you can't avoid this step even if you're the most outgoing dude at the party. Here are several ways to construct your network:

1. **Start with people you know**: People who know you well will be your greatest advocates. They are the ones who will keep their eyes open for potential jobs and will introduce you powerfully to their network. These folks are the easiest to approach, and the most likely to connect you to multiple people.

2. **Connect with your friends' networks**: Building connections at a second ("friend of a friend") or third degree of separation greatly expand your potential contacts. Ask each of your friends for names of three people they know who they recommend you speak with during your search. They don't need to have a job to

fill. You're looking for information or contacts to aid you on your journey.

3. **Use LinkedIn® to turbo-charge your network:** LinkedIn® is a public company that runs the largest professional networking site on the Internet, with over 135 million members. Think of it as a social network for business, careers, and job search. LinkedIn® is a terrific job search resource that you need to add to your toolkit. We'll discuss this in more detail below.

4. **Network through groups with which you have an affiliation:** These might include your college, church, clubs, and so on. Most universities have regional alumni groups you could join. Go to the social functions at your church, talk to everyone you can find, and collect business cards as appropriate. Ditto for your hobbies. There's a group for nearly everything and you never know who those members will know.

5. **Join industry or functional groups that are specifically organized for networking:** Do you want to work in San Diego at a biotech firm? Check out the San Diego Biotechnology Network at www.sdbn.org. How about Public Relations? See www.prsa.org. Check out the National Human Resources Association at www.humanresources.org if you are an HR professional. Do you aspire to be a working Santa Claus? Then try the Amalgamated Order of Real Bearded Santas™ at www.aorbsinc.com. We could go on for multiple pages with organizations devoted to serving members in specific industries, functional areas (like human resources, marketing, engineering, etc.), and geographies. Do a Google search on the appropriate keywords and see what you find. Ask people in your network for other ideas on organizations that might be appropriate to your target industry and job.

6. **Find groups whose purpose is to help members with job search:** You will find numerous organizations that help job searchers network. They may offer seminars on resume writing, interviewing, and other useful subjects. More importantly, organizations like these help expand your network of contacts that may lead you to a job. Look for groups local to the geography where you intend to find work. Some people hesitate to hang out with other job searchers, feeling competitive with them. Get over it! Job seekers help each other find jobs faster, not slower. And, your job-seeking peers will have more patience

with your job search ups and downs than will your employed friends.

Networking takes time, and when connecting with groups, it often takes money, too. Make the best use of your time and money. With potential networking groups, look at their websites. Check to see that they have regular meetings. Call or email the contact person and inquire how many active members they have and how many of those members typically attend the meetings. Finally, beware of going to functions where you have little interest in the subject being discussed. You'll be bored and won't engage as easily with those who are there. Focus on subjects you are passionate about. Your conversations will be livelier and you'll present yourself in a better light to potential job search contacts.

Susan Penn, Vice President of HR, suggests the following:

"Follow the 'Rules of Attraction.' By that I mean find out what professional groups meet in your community that provide information that interests you. Then attend. This will provide a learning experience with individuals who are working in areas you are interested in while affording the opportunity to network and discuss your interests with future professional contacts. Get business cards and follow up. Building relationships is what it's all about. Often one person will lead to the next, providing invaluable connections within your community and helpful information regarding new business developments and opportunities.

Be a learner. Ask questions rather than feeling you need to know the answers. Many established business leaders appreciate being able to demonstrate their expertise, and will be impressed by someone who asks rather than gives an elevator speech."

LinkedIn®: The Network Accelerator

LinkedIn® is an essential part of a professional job search. It enables you to easily connect with people you know and from there to gain introductions to people they know. Even if you're not a math geek, you can quickly see that this approach rapidly adds exponentially more contacts to your network. Here are a few ways that you can use LinkedIn® to help you in your search:

- Determine whether someone you know is connected to an individual in a company in which you have an interest

- Find people of similar skills, experience, and/or geographic locale
- Prior to an interview, view the public profiles of the people with whom you will be speaking to better understand what they do, formulate questions for them, and find possible areas of common interest
- After you get hired, look at the profiles of your new colleagues to give you a better perspective on their skills and experience, which may be helpful to you in your new job.

To establish an account with LinkedIn®, visit **www.linkedin.com**. Once on the site, do the following:

1. **Set up your profile**. It's best you do this before you start networking. Update it again as soon as your resume is finalized. Your LinkedIn® profile contains similar information, so you'll want to give careful thought to what you put here. Another benefit to having a completed resume is that you can use the LinkedIn® resume importer to help you build your profile. We recommend shortening the resume content a bit for LinkedIn®. Think pithy and sound bites. Also, think carefully about the descriptor you choose to place right under your name. We recommend using a title that describes what you're looking for rather than "Job Seeker" or, heaven forbid, "Unemployed."

2. **Add your contacts**. Take the list you brainstormed earlier and use the "Add Connections" feature to send invitations to connect. (Hint: You can upload all your contacts to LinkedIn® through a variety of email or other contact databases.) We strongly suggest sending a customized invitation to each person. This is a great way to alert your network about what you're looking for. Each individual will need to accept your invitation before that person will show up as a connection of yours. Once that happens, you'll be able to see who's connected to each of your contacts.

3. **Give and ask for recommendations**. Go to "Profile>Request Recommendations" and recommend people you know and respect, and in turn ask for recommendations from them and other selected people who know you. Obvious good examples are those with whom (and for whom) you've worked and former professors or teachers. Bad examples might include people who hate your guts and drinking buddies who have no idea of your skills beyond your ability to put down copious shots of tequila. Your goal is to give someone who is

viewing your profile a snapshot of who you are, your skills and experience, and what it's like to work with you.

While we're on the subject of online profiles and social media, there's one more thing worth mentioning. Many potential employers will look at your social media presence on Facebook, Twitter, Tumblr, or any other online service they can find. Clean those up! Most bosses won't be real excited about adding a hard-partying, foul-mouthed person to their staff. A racy social media presence increases the odds that your resume will make a quick trip to the dreaded corporate recycle bin.

How to Make Great Connections

Once you have your LinkedIn® profile set up, it's time to start networking. Since your first degree contacts are the people you already know, that's the place to begin. We recommend a phone call to each individual. Even if you get voicemail, you can convey your enthusiasm better with your voice than in email. Explain the reason for the call and ask if you can talk to them for 30 minutes at a location that is convenient for them. It's best to set up in-person meetings, if possible. Coffee shops are great venues. If you got voicemail, follow up with an email giving potential dates you are available and locations convenient to them.

At the meeting, don't open the conversation with, "I'm looking for a job. Have you heard of any?" Instead, you need to engage their mind and heart into helping you. Describe your passions and skills. Talk about your ideal job using the criteria you developed earlier. Request their opinions, advice, and ideas. Ask them to help you brainstorm companies, possible roles, and people with you. Kim Box, a former Vice President at Hewlett-Packard, told us that,

> "Early in my career, I didn't realize the power of stating what you wanted. When I realized that I needed to make it known that I wanted to reach a certain position and I engaged with the people who could make it happen, that's when I started to create my own destiny instead of waiting for it to happen."

If the person you are meeting with comes up with names of people, ask if you can use his or her name when contacting these folks. Hopefully, they'll volunteer to make an email or phone introduction for you. If not, do it yourself. Your goal is to get at least three contact names from each person. Manage the meeting so that you keep the time commitment you made earlier. If you promised 30 minutes, make sure you are finished in 30 minutes. Afterwards, be sure to send a thank you note, even if it's your best buddy.

The next step is to connect with the second-degree referred contacts from the meetings you had with the people you know. Compose an email that looks something like this:

> "_____ referred me to you. He/she thought you would be a good person to brainstorm with about my job search and to give me your advice about _____ (or your perspective on _____ industry or your opinion of the companies in _____ industry). Would you be available to meet for 30 minutes next week at a place that's convenient for you?"

You can also use the phone to make initial contact. If you get voicemail, leave a message that alerts them to your coming email.

During your meetings, never ask about job openings, unless you know of a specific one at their company for which you are well qualified. Ask for information and introductions. Your goal in these conversations is to get a referral into any of the companies on your target list. (See Chapter 10 for details.) Also, you should ask for three more names of people you could contact, with the same request to use the referrer's name. Again, at the end of the meeting, send a thank you note—email is okay.

Now for some great news: After you have met with an individual on your "second degree" contact list, they move onto your "first degree" contact list since you now know them personally. Request a connection with them on LinkedIn®.

Like the shampoo bottle says, "Lather, rinse, and repeat." Use this process with every person in your contact list. Odds are good that someone in your ever-growing network has a direct contact into one of your target companies or to a specific hiring manager. By following this process for as long as it takes, you'll learn a great deal about the industry you're interested in as well as the specific companies on your list. You'll also build a great network that you'll be able to nurture for the future.

Networking Events

Nearly every town and city of decent size has a plethora of organizations that sponsor events where people of specific industries and careers can network with each other. Industry groups, non-profits, and professional recruiters are examples of groups that typically host these events. You may hear about these in some of your networking conversations. Occasionally you'll find mention of them in LinkedIn® if you have joined affiliated industry groups. You can also Google the name of your profession and industry with the name of your geographical area. The search results should return several events of interest that will be attended by people employed in your profession.

If you're new to attending networking events, here are a few tips to make yourself comfortable:

- Know that almost everyone in the world feels a bit awkward walking into a networking event.
- If you have a friend who is interested in attending the same event, fine. Just don't stick together like barnacles the entire time.
- Whether you are alone or not, find someone who is alone to chat with. The line at the bar is often an easy place to strike up a conversation.
- When beginning the conversation, ask about them first. Be interested and curious. Wait for them to ask about you.
- When they do ask about you, have your concise description of what you're looking for in mind, but make it sound spontaneous and unstructured. You could even follow it directly with a question. For example, "I'm Pat Smith. I recently graduated from Kansas State and am looking to utilize my love of sports and writing in the PR field. Who do you think the top five PR firms are in town?"
- Above all, just be human and interested in them. If you try too hard to impress, it can come off as cocky or self-absorbed. Humor is a huge plus!
- Exchange business cards if it feels appropriate and if there's a reason to follow up.
- When you are finished talking with someone, you don't need an excuse to move on. Just say, "Nice chatting with you," shake hands, and walk away.

A Few Final Thoughts on Networking

If you started out with "only" 40 people on your first degree contact list, you will have 160 people in your network if you successfully get three names from each person on your list. The more people you meet, the faster your network will grow, and the sooner you'll get a job. The time investment can be significant, but will be well worth it. In our combined 60 working years, nearly all of the positions we've found have been via our networks of friends and colleagues. We've also met some truly wonderful people along the way.

Use the "It's who you can get to know" maxim to your benefit. People who know you will be terrific advocates and help you get in the door. Once the door is opened, the "what you know" becomes paramount.

CHAPTER 9

INFORMATIONAL INTERVIEWING

"Judge a man by his questions rather than his answers."
- VOLTAIRE

Informational interviewing is an important part of your job search toolkit. It is distinctly different from a formal job interview in purpose, tone, and approach. Unlike a traditional interview, your primary objective is to gather information rather than interviewing for a specific job. If you master this process, your search will be faster and more productive. Informational interviews are useful for:

1. Learning more about a particular industry or industries;
2. Getting to know what a particular job is like;
3. Practicing interviewing skills;
4. Obtaining introductions to people who may lead you forward in your search.

Informational interviewing is a fabulous way to get the "inside scoop" on what's going on. We all have aspirations to do something to change the world, find work that is fun and interesting, and maybe make a ton of money in the process. A set of well-designed informational interviews will help you assess how closely real life aligns with your dreams.

Expected Results

With informational interviews, you have three goals. The first is to find out everything you can about a target industry. For example, is the industry growing wildly or is it stable? Even worse, is it declining? How cutthroat is the competition? Is revenue concentrated in the hands of a few large players or is it widely dispersed across a variety of smaller competitors? Are companies hiring broadly? Is there a shortage of skilled talent? The answers to these questions, and others, will help you assess whether a job in this field has plenty of growth or if it's a dog-eat-dog proposition in a declining industry.

Secondly, you want to walk out of an informational interview with a good feel for the details of the job that's of interest. What's a typical day like? How closely does the actual work correlate to what is taught in school? What are the characteristics of a successful incumbent? For this job, do most companies have a variety of entry-level openings for recent college graduates or are they generally seeking people with many years' experience? What does it take to advance in this field?

Finally, you want to end up with at least one introduction to someone else with whom to have an informational interview. (This doesn't always happen, so be open to outcome.) After talking informally with several people doing the job, you'll get a good idea of whether the content and the role seem like a good fit for you. You'll also greatly expand your professional network. Sherri Petro runs her own consulting company. She offers this observation:

> "I find that people genuinely want to help others. Everyone you meet is connected. If you have defined what you want very clearly, tell those that you meet in very concrete terms and you may be surprised at who they know who can assist you."

Finding Someone to Interview

For an industry-related or specific job-related informational interview, you'll need to have selected one or two target industry and job combinations before proceeding. (Please refer back to Chapter 5, "Self-Assessment," for the methodology of doing so.)

Next, it's time to put your network to work. Search LinkedIn® and local industry groups to locate names of individuals to interview. Ideally, you will already have a direct connection to one or more of these people. If some of the names turn out to be second or third level contacts, use your LinkedIn® network to arrange a connection through a mutual acquaintance.

For a job-related informational interview, you need to have selected both a target industry and a target job within it. Let's assume, for example, that you want to explore working at a Public Relations (PR) agency focused on high-technology companies. First, Google the term "PR agency job titles" or look on job search sites like Monster.com to find job descriptions that intrigue you. Write down the title or titles. In this case the titles might be PR Coordinator, Account Coordinator, PR Account Executive, and PR Supervisor. Then, use LinkedIn® and other networking groups to find someone with that job title or something close to it in your geographic area.

During your self-assessment, you may have selected a business functional area you'd like to work in, but are open as to industry. (Examples of business functions include: marketing, sales, R&D, engineering, finance, manufacturing, information technology, quality, operations, and human resources.) If this is true for you, then find people doing those jobs in a variety of industries to compare and contrast. For example, if you want to work in finance, find people with finance-related job descriptions across several different industries to help narrow your industry preferences.

Ideally, in either industry or job-related informational interviews, try for a direct referral by a mutual acquaintance. Other affiliations are also useful, such as membership in the same group. Examples include alumni of a certain college, fellow surfers, and so on. Also consider joining a LinkedIn® group and use that mutual interest. Just be sure that your group membership is based on a legitimate interest on your part.

Lastly, find non-profit groups in your area that exist to support job seekers. Sometimes these organizations have lists of people who have specifically volunteered to be available for informational interviews. If you have a good idea of industry and job titles, you can quickly get connected to a willing interviewee.

Keys to Success

Even though the terms "job interview" and "informational interview" sound similar, the purpose and approach are quite different. It's important to recognize the distinctions and follow proper etiquette. Once you've found a person to interview, the keys to effective informational interviewing are:

- Figure out a way to ask genuinely and respectfully for someone's time. After all, you may only be kicking tires and find out you dislike this particular job or industry.

- Ask only for 30 minutes and respect that time. If they want to go longer, fine. If they don't offer longer, end the meeting exactly at 30 minutes.
- With only 30 minutes, you need to be prepared. Develop a set of questions and rank them, with highest priority questions first. That way, if you run out of time, the less important questions can be skipped. To help you, we have provided sample questions below.
- Be insatiably curious! Open-ended questions are best. For example, ask, "What do you like about your job?" rather than, "Do you like your job?" Ask follow up questions, as appropriate.
- Always send a thank-you note or email for their time. Summarize what you learned and thank them for their insights.
- Connect to them on LinkedIn®. If you do this before your interview, you can tailor your questions to each individual's work experience and interests. You can also see who they know for possible introductions.
- Keep them apprised of your progress every month or when there is significant news.
- Let them know where you end up. If it's someone you want to keep in touch with, invite him or her to lunch as a thank-you. (And pick up the tab, okay?)

Remember that the person you are interviewing is doing you a favor. Handle the process with respect and professionalism. Your efforts at doing this will be noticed and appreciated. When you eventually find a job, pay it forward by making yourself available to other job seekers.

Assembling Your Questions

If you are lucky, your target industries will be related so that you get perspective on each from the same individual. For example, let's say you are interested in biotech, pharmaceuticals, and healthcare. You could do informational interviews with people in each of these industries and ask each person to compare and contrast the three, since they are closely related.

Even if your target set of industries is seemingly unrelated, look for possible connections. One of your targets might be a customer or supplier to the others, for example. By examining industry connections, you will get a better perspective on how each operates and will maximize the value you get from each interview. Construct your questions accordingly.

To help you get started, here are some industry-related questions we have found useful. Review this list, then add your own:

- How did you get started in this industry?
- What made you choose this career?
- What do you see as the future prospects of this industry? How does that compare to _____ and _____ industry?
- If you were to do it over again, would you choose this industry? Why or why not?
- What makes this field unique?
- What's the best thing about this industry? Worst?
- What types of people excel in this line of work?
- How important are advanced degrees in this industry? In what functions?
- What are typical career paths in this field?
- How active are you in industry-related groups? What benefits do you get from that?
- What advice do you have for someone like me considering this industry?
- What other people might be good informational sources about this industry?

Preparing a list of questions aimed at specific job titles is a similar process. You'll easily generate a bunch of these after you've researched job descriptions for positions in which you have an interest. Here are some sample job-related questions:

- Why did you join this industry? This company? In this role?
- What's been your biggest surprise so far?
- What skills do you use the most?
- What skills are totally necessary?
- What parts of the job do you like the most? The least?
- If you could do it over again, what career would you pick? Why?
- What does a great day look like? An average day?
- What's your biggest frustration in this job?
- What does the career path look like?
- If you had it to do over again, what would you have liked to know about this field?
- What advice do you have for people considering this role?

- What other people might be good informational sources about this type of job?

Informational interviews are also a great place to ask some of the questions you wouldn't want to bring up in a regular job interview. (Be careful here. You might end up interviewing with this company eventually. But still, given that the meeting is set up as an informational interview, you do have a fair amount of leeway.) Questions you might want to ask, depending on what's important to you, include:

- What are the salary ranges for the various job titles?
- How is the work/life balance?
- How would you rate this company/industry in terms of flexibility for working parents (or triathletes or whatever)?
- What's the company culture like?
- How much opportunity is there for creativity?

If you ask every question we've listed above, you will not finish the interview within the timeframe you promised. And that's not even counting the questions you added. Carefully prune and prioritize the list so that your essential questions are addressed within the agreed-upon time.

Wrapping Up

At the end of an informational interview, always ask, "Who else do you recommend I have an informational interview with to learn more about this industry (or job title)?" Don't ask about any open jobs at their company or others. If you do that, you are indicating that the whole premise of your meeting was a thinly veiled sham. The person you are speaking to will volunteer this information if they know of any open jobs and have been impressed with you. Lastly, at the end of your meeting, be sure to ask sincerely what you can do for them.

We recommend that you do at least three informational interviews before deciding to pursue jobs in a given industry or function. You'll be better informed about the position and you'll know better questions to ask in actual job interviews. Hopefully, the people you have met will also network you into some open jobs. The discovery process during these interviews will help narrow your path to one that feels congruent with what you want.

At the end of an informational interview, you can deem it a success if any of the following occur:

- You are more informed about the job and industry. Even if you don't like what you heard, it's still a win. It's better to invest 30 minutes in a conversation and discover a job's not what you think it would be than to take a position in that field and find out later that you hate it.
- You feel you have a new friend or mentor.
- You have one or more names of additional people to contact.

Here's one personal example of how this process was helpful. Lauren had an informational interview with a mergers and acquisitions (M&A) consulting firm. She found out the work looked something like this:

1. Endless researching to find target companies.
2. Often, targets get shot down by potential acquirers, so back to step #1.
3. If a target is pursued, drop everything, work 18+ hour days for 3-4 weeks with lots of travel.
4. There is at best a 20% chance the deal will get completed. So, most of the time, all that work is for naught.

While some people would thrive in this environment, Lauren thought it looked like a serious hairball and moved on to other possibilities. With relief!

Informational interviewing is a relatively low-pressure technique for learning about a particular industry or job title, practicing interviewing skills, and expanding your network of professional contacts. Have fun with it! The more you do, the easier they become. Even better, informational interviews will help you build a list of companies you want to target for your ideal job. Let's talk about that next.

CHAPTER 10

TARGET COMPANY LIST

"A company is known by the people it keeps."
– HARRY KLINGER

By now you've narrowed down to one or two job/industry combinations. Next, you'll make it more concrete by compiling a target list of companies within that industry or industries. This list is composed of potential employers who meet the job criteria you specified in Chapter 6. These firms have employees in the job titles you want, a good set of benefits, a culture that fits your values, are within your desired geographic area, and meet other essential criteria. You'll discover these companies through research, word-of-mouth, and informational interviews.

The target company list you will create offers several benefits. First, you'll be better able to focus your time on employers that have already met your criteria. Better focus equates to more efficient use of your time because you'll be aiming at pre-approved targets. For example, you can add those companies to your "follow" list on LinkedIn®, set up specific criteria within the major job listing sites so you'll be alerted to any new job opportunities, and keep tabs on their websites and other related activities.

Second, a target list enables you to leverage your network effectively. A LinkedIn® search will quickly show to whom you are connected within those companies. From there, you can arrange informational interviews as appropriate.

Third, your target list gives you a reason to reconnect with folks you met with earlier in your search. Reconnecting reminds people you're still looking and helps them think of specific people to whom they can introduce you within these companies. And of course, you will use your target list with new connections as well.

Compiling the List

The procedure for building up your list is straightforward, though the time investment may be significant. We'd suggest starting with the industry (or industries) on the focus list you created earlier. From there, apply each of your significant objective criteria against information available from public research sources. Typical forms of objective data might include things like company size (revenues or employees), geographic location, and benefit offerings.

It may be possible to move a few of your subjective criteria into the "objective" category with a bit of creativity. For example, if a robust training program is important to you, consider focusing on larger companies, as those are the most likely to have the required resources. Similarly, if you want a company known for its great working environment, you can look at employees' comments at sites like Glassdoor.com or Google the phrase "Best places to work" to find companies that have been called out for success in this area.

You'll find a wealth of online databases, industry periodicals, and local business publications to help locate specific companies in your target industry that meet your criteria. Here are some tips on getting value from each of those:

- **Online databases**: Most public libraries are now connected to several online research databases. Choose a business database or directory of companies. Use the database's advanced search capability that allows you to select ranges on more than one variable. Using your objective criteria, search for target companies in your industry of choice. If you are considering more than one industry, run each search separately. For example, if you're looking for internet marketing companies, Chicago metro area, company size 50 employees or greater, you should come up with a list of companies that is manageable— roughly 25 or fewer firms. Should the resulting list be longer than that, think about how to narrow it further via objective criteria. Avoid doing detailed research on a much longer list.

You want to actually find a job, as opposed to using all your time doing research. So, in the above example, you could add criteria of "X" miles from your zip code of residence in the Chicago area to narrow the choices.

- **Industry periodicals**: These publications frequently compile lists of companies in their industry. Often these are national in scope. However, if there's an online version, they may offer a search feature to narrow to your desired area. The benefit of industry publications is more specificity within the industry. For example, if you are interested in software companies, an industry periodical will likely break them down by product niche, industry served, business vs. consumer, and so on.

- **Local business publications**: Many major metro areas have business journals or other local business publications. In our area, the *San Diego Business Journal* is a leading example. These publishers often have industry lists already compiled. If they require a subscription to access their online sources, it may be worth buying. Reading these periodicals is a great way to keep up on local business news and companies that are hiring.

Once you have about 25 companies on your target list sorted by industry, it's time to begin detailed research.

First, we suggest you show your list to people you know who have been active in the local business community for a number of years. Sales people, accountants, attorneys, and consultants are especially good sources as they may have had direct contact with many companies in the area. Again, use your network. Even if your network isn't huge yet, think creatively. The people you need to speak with may be friends of your parents or even your parents. What about your parents' accountant or attorney, for example? You may be surprised to find how many people are available and willing to help.

These conversations will help you refine your list by addressing your subjective criteria. What reputation does each of these companies have? What are they like to work for? What's the company culture? Look back at your ideal job criteria, and see what else you want to ask about.

Second, set up informational interviews with people you know or can get connected with who work for any of the target companies now or have in the recent past. You can easily find these connections using LinkedIn®. Go to the closest connections first. Ask the same questions as above, and add in queries only an employee would know. What kind of people fit in and don't? What does it take to excel and get promoted? What opportunities are there for training, outside courses, and tuition reimbursement? How flexible are the work hours? Are budgets tight or is there room for hiring? How's the cafeteria food?

It's especially nice to ask some of these questions to a peer or someone in a department other than the one in which you'd like to work, rather than trying to get the inside scoop as part of a formal job interview. If you like what you hear, work on getting an introduction into the hiring manager of your desired department. Do this even if there are no published job openings. You never know when spots will open up. When one does, you want to already have your foot in the door. Even better, managers can sometimes create either a permanent spot or an internship if they meet someone they think is excellent.

Finally, show your target list to anyone you are meeting (or have met with) in the course of your networking and informational interviewing. This is a great way to spur people's thoughts on how they can help you. If you're connected with them on LinkedIn®, you already have visibility to their network. Research their connections and request appropriate introductions. One assertive 20-something that Lauren coached said if he had to do his job search over again he'd, "cold call every company on my target list. I'd bug them weekly until they met with me!" He was very clear he wanted to work for one of these firms and would do whatever it took to get a meeting with one or more of them.

Your object in this refinement process is to rule out companies that are not a fit. This frees up time to focus on those firms that look like a good match. Avoid pruning the list excessively. If you're looking at large companies in a growing industry, aim for at least seven to ten targets. If you are focusing on smaller firms, the list may need to be up to twice as long. No matter how good your research, there are other companies out there that will be a good fit for you. Stay open to new possibilities.

It may feel counterintuitive to take companies off your list. In doing so you may feel your chances of getting hired just declined. In reality, the probability of finding a position at a firm you are attracted to actually improves as you dump those that are poor fits. Remember the paradox of job search. By narrowing your focus and being specific, others will be better able to help you find something you really want.

Your target list will change over time. While you may rule some out, others will emerge as candidates during the course of your search. As you get interviews and eventually offers, you will naturally focus down towards the one you will eventually choose.

CHAPTER 11

SUSTAINING YOUR SEARCH

"No bees, no honey, no work, no money."
– PROVERB

Job search is not an easy process. Basically your "job" during a search is to create possibilities for yourself, put positive energy out there to find opportunities, and inspire others to help you in that process. These three tasks require large amounts of energy, enthusiasm, confidence, perseverance, and faith on your part. You may need to sustain this level of effort for quite a while.

The process will have plenty of ups and downs. It'll sometimes be exciting and exhilarating. At other times, job search will be tiring, draining, and probably discouraging. Let's look at some techniques for managing your search without running out of steam.

Amount of Time to Spend on Your Search

Because you are in the business of generating possibilities, you need to exude energy in all your interactions. Whether you are working or not, you cannot realistically spend 40 or more hours a week on your search and do it effectively. At the same time, you need to put in enough hours to sustain forward momentum. For those who are currently employed or are full-time students, 5 to 10 hours per week is probably realistic for job search.

If you are unemployed, we'd suggest you devote at least 20 to 25 hours per week on your search. Barbara Wakefield, a former manager at a large high-tech company, currently does career coaching for young adults. She is even more blunt, telling us that:

> "When you are searching for a job, you should work hard at it. It just kills me the number of 20-somethings I coach these days that put in an application here and there, and then stop. Sheesh! If you are unemployed, there isn't any reason you can't work several hours a day either submitting resumes, customizing cover letters, practicing interview skills, informational interviewing, driving around to companies trying to get to meet someone face-to-face, whatever. It takes hard work and creativity to find work!"

So, whatever amount of time you allot to your job search, set a realistic schedule and keep to it. You may decide to set a number of phone calls and emails you are going to make each day. Even better is to focus on getting a certain number of face-to-face appointments per week. You may want to set designated job search hours as well. Think about a structure that works for you and then make it happen.

How to Spend Your Job Search Time

Many people spend way too much time responding to job openings they find on the Internet. Once your resume and cover letter are complete it's an easy thing to do. You also get to avoid putting yourself out there on the phone or in person with another human being. Is it time well spent? Sadly, the answer is "no."

Only a very small number of online applications yield a response, including even an acknowledgement of receipt or, "Thanks, but no thanks." Your resume is happily cavorting with thousands of others in cyberspace without helping you land a job.

Once you have completed your self-assessment, job criteria, and resume, about 80% of your job search time should be spent on informational interviews and networking. (The higher you progress in your career, the bigger the networking percentage gets.) In all likelihood you will get your next job by talking to people who know people who know people who have open jobs.

Reserve only 10% of your job search time for online applications and another 10% for research and preparation for interviews. Get away from your computer. Get out there and spend time with people who can help you find your next job! When you're interacting with people during your search, Cláudia Schwartz recommends that you:

"Live every day as though each interaction with someone (including yourself) is a preparation for a job interview. Act as if an agent of your dream employer was watching you now. It probably is true since most jobs come through the connections with people who know us. Remember: It's not just 'who you know' that gets you the job you want. More importantly, it is 'who knows you' and how you work."

Rewards and Reinforcement

It's no small feat to stay positive during job search. You never know when some exciting job is going to come up, when someone will respond to your request for time, or when you'll get an interview call-back. It can be very frustrating not to have control of the process or timing.

Staying positive is especially challenging for the unemployed. It can be difficult to remain upbeat when the bills are coming due with no inbound cash to help pay them. However, job search does provide the gift of time, particularly for those not working concurrently. If you have done your four or five hours of job search today, you could be done by noon and get to play for the afternoon. You have time to think, visit with people you care about, be creative or do hobbies, exercise, read, learn, do volunteer work, and so on. Too many people squander the gift of time during job search by waiting for calls or emails and living in anxiety. Don't let this happen to you.

Think about what you've always wanted to do, but haven't had time. Maybe now is a great opportunity to learn a foreign language, play an instrument, or take a course on something you've always wanted to learn. Work/life balance is something you want to have during job search as well as when you're employed. Start enjoying it now.

Similarly, create rewards and reinforcement to help you sustain your job search. Tie them to the completion of specific activities. For example, if you successfully schedule three informational interviews, reward yourself by taking the rest of the day off, go to an afternoon movie, or anything else that you consider fun or relaxing.

Don't hesitate to also reward yourself for accomplishing smaller things. For example, if you are intimidated about calling a particular contact, decide in advance to treat yourself after successfully doing it. If budget is a problem, find inexpensive or free things to do that satisfy your fun criteria, like having a picnic, taking a walk, or going to a museum on its free day. Create your own list of small rewards, indulgences, and activities you enjoy. Having a goal tied with reinforcement can help you push forward when your motivation or enthusiasm is flagging.

Spend Time with Others

Job search can be a solitary process, particularly if you don't have other group activities to fill your time during the day. To avoid turning into a hermit, we recommend hanging out with other people who are in the same boat. Find compatriots who are organized, upbeat, and diligent. Avoid the perpetual whiners and complainers. The attitudes of those around you are infectious.

With your employed friends, be judicious about how much you discuss your search. Give them quick, regular updates. Be attentive to whether they are asking questions or not. If not, be short and succinct. The most important thing to keep sharing is your description of what you are looking for, especially as you refine it over time.

Job search can be a great time to make new friends. Who knows? Maybe you'll meet your future spouse or life partner during this period. After all, you are meeting lots of new people and you have more time. When Lauren thinks about her closest friends, she finds that an amazing number of them were people she met during one of her job searches. She was more vulnerable and approachable, less busy, and made the time for new people in her life.

Take a Vacation

During your search, there's no harm in taking short vacations that are consistent with your financial situation. In fact, long weekends in new surroundings could help recharge your batteries. The early days of your job quest tend to be the best time to be away. You're still working on your self-assessment and figuring out what you want to do. Time away from home is a wonderful opportunity to think about your passions, interests, and skills in a relaxed setting.

Vacations become a bit trickier once job opportunities begin to be generated by your network. During this period, we'd be hesitant to be away for more than a few days. While you can stay in touch easily by email and cell phone, you run the risk of losing momentum by being gone for extended periods.

Good and Bad Job Search Times of the Year

You may have heard a variety of myths as to the optimal time of year to job search. We've heard comments like, "Nothing happens between Thanksgiving and New Year," and "July and August are slow hiring months." Forget all these bromides. Here's what we've found to be true:

- People get hired throughout the year. You are looking for only one job and that could happen anytime. You never know when something will show up, so don't slack off during alleged "slow periods."
- In the summer, while an appointment may have to be scheduled well in advance due to vacation, once the appointment is on the calendar the person is less likely to reschedule and is more likely to give you additional time. Typically, fewer meetings are held in the summer months at many companies, so the person tends to be more available the times they are in the office.
- Between Christmas and New Year's, if you phone or email and find someone at their desk, you can often get an appointment, sometimes immediately. It's also a great time to try a random "show up at a company and see who you can meet" visit. There is so little going on that people may enjoy a fresh face to break the tedium of cleaning out files and getting ready for the New Year.

There are lots of excuses for not being in active job search mode. The ones about time of year are basically rubbish. The only valid reason for delaying an active (outreaching) search is that you are still doing the work to figure out what you really want to do. So, finish that and get going.

Budget for Networking Events and Lunches

If you are in job-search mode, money is a scarce commodity. We get that. We assume you already have a basic infrastructure in place, like appropriate clothing, cell phone, email, and Internet access. However, you'll need to plan on a few other expenses unique to job search. The common items are networking events and lunches.

Guidelines on networking events

- Research the organization thoroughly before attending an event with a significant fee. How many members are there? How many typically show up at an event? Call the Executive Director if you can't find the answers online. Ensure that enough people will be attending to make it worth the expense.
- If it sounds too expensive, it is. Pass on it and find another way to meet those people. If money is an issue, only attend if you are interested in the content as well as the people you might meet. That way, if you don't meet anyone who can help you with your search, at least you'll have received some value from the presentation.
- See if anyone in your network will be there to facilitate introductions at events you choose to attend.
- Research the membership list in advance. Some organizations also give a handout of attendees at registration. Know in advance whom you want to meet.
- Ask each person you talk to at an event whether they might be able to introduce you to one or two others who are also present (more would be presumptuous).

Lunches and coffees

- If expenses are a huge issue, opt for meeting people in their offices during the workday for informational interviews. (Employers will pick up the tab during formal interview lunches, so no worries there.)
- Meeting for coffee or tea is a low-cost alternative. Offer to pay for both of you, if possible.
- If lunch is the best time for the person to meet, select a reasonably priced restaurant. Avoid fast food establishments. Sometimes the other person will offer to pay. If they do, accept graciously, but promise (and hold to it!) that you'll treat them once you have a job.

Decorum

This should go without saying, but be very careful about imbibing during networking events. Nothing can sour a potential employer more than seeing someone a bit buzzed at an after-work networking event. It's best to stick with water or soda. Also, be sure to dress professionally.

Keep the Ball Rolling

While we wish you a quick and easy job search, you should plan on a potentially lengthy process. Once you get rolling, keep going. Do whatever you can to make job search a fun and interesting time for you. Create those possibilities for a job you love and send that positive energy into the world. (Sorry, we're from California so we had to say that.) Take care of yourself during the process and hang in there. Something good will happen when you least expect it.

CHAPTER 12

INTERVIEWING

"When you are asked if you can do a job, tell 'em,
'Certainly I can!' Then, get busy and find out how to do it."
– THEODORE ROOSEVELT

Jim landed his first professional job interview in the spring of his senior year. College graduation was fast approaching. Having grown up in snowy Vermont, he decided he was done with the bitter cold winters. He focused on companies in California, hoping to live the life of surf and sun. At the time, companies based on the West Coast didn't recruit in New England in great numbers, so campus interview options were scarce. After several weeks of striking out, a surprise phone call (based only on sending an unsolicited resume) from a respected multinational company resulted in an offer for an interview at the company's offices in the San Francisco Bay Area. Jackpot! The corporate travel desk called the next day to arrange the trip. When Jim told the agent he'd be traveling from Burlington, Vermont, the reaction from the travel desk was, "Do they have an airport?" Ugh. This was not an encouraging start.

By the time you are done with your interviews, you will also have some good stories to tell. And you will learn a lot. Corporate cultures are as diverse as the people that populate them. You will meet some great people and perhaps a few windbags. You will be exposed to some amazing new ideas and products. You may also see some places that are as dull as dishwater.

The purpose of this chapter is to help prepare you for both telephone and in-person interviews. Once you've reached this stage, you should be proud that you have stood out from the crowd well enough to be one of the few in consideration for a particular position. This chapter will help increase the probability that a job offer is made to you, rather than one of your competitors.

The Phone Screen

The first step in the interview process is often a phone screen. When you get to this point, your odds have improved dramatically. From a pile of dozens of resumes (or more), the employer has whittled the list down to perhaps ten to fifteen people that look like a potential fit for an opening. You may hear from a hiring manager, a member of the HR staff, or possibly someone else on the team. The employer's goal during this step is to prune the list down to four or five people to invite for an in-person interview. Your goal, of course, is to be on that list.

Be ready for a call out of the blue. Most phone screens are scheduled, but it's possible the caller may ask if you have time available "right now" to talk. You may not even remember sending your resume to this employer. When the caller self-identifies as a potential employer, you need to switch into your most professional phone mode immediately. In fact, while you're in your job search, it's best to always answer your phone professionally if you don't recognize the inbound phone number. A pleasant and upbeat, "Hi, this is _____" will suffice. Make sure your voicemail greeting is similarly professional. Eliminate all background noise, ideally, before you answer the call. If you're on a mobile phone, check to see that you have good reception before you answer. And of course, if you're driving, pull over! Cláudia Schwartz, a Principal at HR Results, says,

> "If you get a call from a potential employer or from someone who can help you get a job, stop what you are doing and find a way to give the person your full, professional attention. Don't say you are having dinner with friends and ask the person to call you back. Quite a few candidates have moved down my priority list for doing that."

If you're truly unable to talk when the call arrives, take the initiative to propose another time within the next 24 hours. Don't hang up without obtaining the person's name, direct phone number, and company name. It's also handy to get a brief outline of the job and other highlights to help you prepare for the conversation. Diane, a Vice President of HR, offers this advice:

"Always ask for an in-person meeting if you can do it. Phone screens are just that—the objective is to screen you, mostly out. Go in and make eye contact if you can. When I've been a phone screen candidate, I have often told the person setting up the phone meeting that I would be glad to come in and they were fine about it."

When the phone discussion begins, have an environment that is calm, relaxed, and allows you to think without distraction. A phone screen typically runs 20 to 30 minutes, so you won't have much time to make a good impression. Be ready with answers to questions about the type of job you're after, key experiences on your resume, and relevant academic coursework.

During the conversation, offer crisp, direct answers to the questions you're asked. You may find it helpful to stand up as you talk. Your voice will sound more powerful and confident if you do. Avoid drilling down into lots of detail unless the caller requests it. Don't overly embellish your accomplishments. Be honest and forthright if you aren't experienced in a particular area.

Good phone screeners will give you an opportunity to ask questions as well, especially if they like what they hear from you earlier in the conversation. Use this as an opportunity to find out more about the company and the job opening. This will help you decide if you want to move forward to a formal interview and will also help you prepare for it.

When the conversation concludes, there are a limited number of potential outcomes. The best alternative is an invitation for an in-person interview. If the phone screener is enthusiastic, you may get an invitation on the spot. It's also possible that the hiring manager still has many phone screens to conduct and will be unable to let you know where you stand right away. Generally, though, you should at least get a decent feel before the call is over. Before hanging up, make sure you ask when the decision will be made and what the process will be.

If it's clear that you're not a good match for this job, but you have a strong interest in the company, ask the caller whether there are other jobs closer to your areas of interest and expertise. You should also ask whether the person is on LinkedIn® and whether it would be okay for you to connect. A phone call like this is always an opportunity to expand your professional network.

One of your phone screens will result in a mutual decision to proceed with an in-person interview. So, let's get ready to handle that.

Preparing for the Interview

Prepare for every formal interview the same way you prepare for a university exam. You want to learn everything you can about the company and the job in advance so that you arrive prepared, knowledgeable, and engaged. This involves research, study, and practice for the likely questions you will be asked, and for those you want to ask in return.

The obvious first stop is the company's website. Visit every page, if possible. Learn about the products, culture, HR benefits, and senior leadership. Take notes on your key findings, questions, and concerns. As the website is the company's attempt to look good, you'll also want to look at opinions from other sources. Perform Google searches for customer reviews of the company's products and customer service. Take a look at websites like Glassdoor.com to view opinions that employees have about their company. How does customer and employee feedback jibe with the perky verbiage on the company website?

Check your LinkedIn® network to see whether anyone you know has contacts inside the company. Talk to those people. Also talk to people who have left the company. Find out the good, bad, and ugly. Try to get a sense for the company's reputation, how it treats its employees, and what it's like to work there.

When your research is finished, prepare questions that address areas of interest or concern. Similarly, develop responses to potential interview questions that will assess how your skills and experience fit with the company and the open position. Rhonda Rhyne, author of *The Bitch and the Glass Ceiling* and a former CEO, points out that the best queries are about the company and manager and not about you. She suggests the following set of questions:

1. "How would you describe the ideal candidate or the top qualities in an ideal candidate?" Use this as an opportunity to dovetail your past successful experiences to these qualities.
2. "How do you envision this position supporting you?" This translates to the fact that you will make the hiring manager's life easier.
3. "How would you define 'success' for this position?" This helps you understand how the company will evaluate your performance and may provide insight into the company's culture.

4. "What are the top three to five areas to immediately address?" This demonstrates a results-oriented focus.
5. "Do you have any concerns about my ability to excel in the position?" This allows you an opportunity to address any perceived shortcomings.
6. "How does this position fit into the company's long-term plans?" This helps you identify how the role fits into the company's long-term strategy.
7. "What can I do as follow-up to assist in moving forward as the top candidate?" This demonstrates interest and initiative.

After you've created your question list, practice asking and answering with a friend. Your advance work will help you show up confident, sincere, and professional.

If appropriate, assemble a portfolio of your work that is relevant to the position. Graphic designers, photographers, and writers are among the professionals from whom a portfolio of work is expected. Bring samples of your work that demonstrate your skill and help set you apart from competitors.

Get a good night's sleep the night before the interview and eat a healthy breakfast the next morning. Dress professionally and conservatively, even if you know the company culture is casual. For guys, that means a suit and tie. For the ladies, a dress, suit, or pantsuit that doesn't reveal cleavage or midriff. Solid colors are best. Avoid distracting earrings. Cover tattoos if possible. Wear leather shoes with low heels. Sneakers, flip-flops, and open-toed shoes are out.

Get "psyched-up" before leaving for the interview. Many world-class athletes spend time just before their events visualizing themselves winning. Consider trying this technique. Find a quiet, comfortable place to sit and visualize yourself as the ideal candidate for this job. Think positive messages and ignore the negative thoughts. As you do this, take several breaths to calm yourself. It may sound hokey, but visualization exercises can be quite helpful. (How many gold medalists spend time ahead of the event thinking they suck and are going to come in last? Our guess is none.)

Allow plenty of time to get to the interview location. It's much better to arrive relaxed 15 to 30 minutes early than getting stressed out in traffic before you even begin your meetings. Make sure you have several copies of your resume, your set of questions, and a professional-looking notebook. When you arrive, mute your cell phone. Make a quick bathroom stop. Arrive at reception about five minutes before your appointed time.

Let the Games Begin

The minute you walk in the door, it's time to put on your game face. Assume that everything you say and do will be observed and assessed until the time you leave the building. Treat everyone with kindness and respect. Even the receptionist may render an opinion of you. Don't underestimate an administrative assistant. They are sometimes among the most powerful people in an office. A smart manager will ask his or her assistant's opinion, knowing that how you treat someone lower on the totem pole says a lot about you.

Similarly, don't sell the HR representative short. We've seen several candidates on their best behavior with other members of the team, who then blow it by not taking the HR person seriously. Big mistake. Human resources people are often among the most seasoned interviewers. The good ones are highly valuable to the hiring manager in offering assessments on likely fit with the organization. They are generally not the ultimate decision-makers, but their vote counts.

Don't forget that you are also being interviewed if you get taken to lunch. While the setting may be informal and relaxed, you are still being evaluated. Use lunch as an occasion to highlight your interpersonal skills. Remember all the table manners that your mother taught you. Don't consume alcoholic beverages. Avoid ordering food that's messy or difficult to eat. Lauren learned this the hard way.

She was once taken on an interview lunch to a nice sushi place. The CEO interviewing her was an intense guy. Big talker. He ordered sushi for both of them. Lauren accidently mixed up the wasabi and soy sauce so strongly that it made her eyes water. As the interviewer was burbling on, all Lauren could think about was the tears in her eyes about to dribble down her cheek. While maintaining eye contact, she reached into her purse for her tissue packet before realizing that she had instead removed a sanitary napkin pouch from her purse. The CEO's eyes looked like they were about to pop out of their sockets. Oops! She did not get a second interview.

Handling Interview Questions

You're going to run into some very skilled interviewers and others who are pathetic. Be prepared for both. Good interviewers focus the majority of their time on open-ended questions that aim to draw out your past experience in a variety of areas. This is called behavioral interviewing. Here are a few examples:

- "Tell me about a time when you used your leadership skills to help resolve a conflict on a team project."
- "Describe a project you completed that was highly complex, requiring many steps to complete. Tell me in detail how you organized it."
- "When have you had the opportunity to use your communication skills to describe a complex topic to someone with little background in that area? What were the results?"

In contrast, a closed-ended question offers little nuance. Here are corresponding closed-ended questions to compare with those listed above:

- "Do you have much leadership experience?"
- "Have you worked on any complex projects?"
- "Have you given many presentations to non-technical audiences?"

Open-ended questions force the candidate to come up with actual experiences that highlight the skill being evaluated. Queries like this are much more effective at helping an interviewer assess strengths and weaknesses than a question that asks for a "yes/no" answer. Open-ended questions are especially helpful in evaluating soft skills such as:

- Teamwork
- Leadership ability
- Verbal communication skills
- Ability to work under pressure
- Dependability
- Work ethic
- Empathy toward others
- Customer service skills

Spend time practicing with sample open-ended behavioral questions ahead of time. (Once again, Google is your friend.) They are tougher to answer than you might think. We've seen many candidates draw a blank the first time they get asked one of these questions. If that happens to you, it's perfectly fine to ask for a minute to think. Interviewers may ask for multiple examples in a given area, so be prepared.

If you have limited work experience, talk about team projects in college if they highlight skill areas that a potential employer would value. Have key vignettes ready as proof points from your resume accomplishments. Demonstrate how you are able to learn quickly with examples from your past. And remember, if you got this far, the hiring manager considers you a serious candidate. Focus on your strengths and confidently outline how you would close any gaps in skills and experience if you are the successful candidate. Sherri Petro runs her own consulting company. She offers this advice:

> "Think from the other side of the desk. What do they want? You are solving a problem for the person who is interviewing you. Most do not enjoy spending hours on end trying to find the right candidate. It's exhausting! Connect the dots very clearly as to why you are the solution to their hiring dilemma."

Pay attention to your body language in every conversation. Lean slightly forward in the chair. Maintain eye contact. Nod occasionally when the other person is speaking to acknowledge that you've heard and understand. And don't forget to smile once in a while! Be yourself and answer honestly and authentically. Former manager Barbara Wakefield shared this story with us:

> "I was interviewing a young college student for a summer position. The only previous experience he had was as a bus boy at a restaurant. I asked him to tell me about his worst experience with a customer and how he handled it. He proceeded to tell me that he fumbled a full tray of dirty dishes and dumped the whole thing on a customer's lap. I could tell he was mortified, so I asked, 'How did you handle it?' He replied very sincerely, 'I ran away and hid.' It just cracked me up! Not that he ran away, but that he was so completely honest in the interview process. We did not end up hiring him, but it was only because we found a more qualified candidate. I would have loved to hire someone who was not afraid to tell the truth in an interview."

Humor can be helpful if it's a natural part of who you are. Just be sure to avoid inappropriate or wise-ass comments. One of our colleagues, who shall remain nameless for this story, is a vivacious redhead and a CEO. She told us she once interviewed a guy and asked her standard question, "What is your biggest weakness?" His reply was, "Redheads." Perhaps he thought he was being funny, but that answer was clearly inappropriate. At a minimum, it demonstrated that he has poor judgment. In the worst case, he's a potential sexual harassment nightmare for his employer. In case it isn't obvious, he didn't get the job.

While most interviews will be one-to-one, some organizations use panel interviews. A panel typically consists of three to six people who take turns asking questions. The idea is that it saves time for all concerned. This format also gives several people the opportunity to observe how you respond, which allows for broader perspective when evaluating all the candidates. (You would be surprised how differently some interviewers react to the identical answer given by a candidate.)

From the candidate's perspective, a panel interview might feel like an inquisition. Five people versus one can be a bit unnerving. To calm your nerves, focus on the person asking the question. Maintain eye contact with the questioner until you've formulated your answer and have begun speaking. When you're about halfway through the answer to a particular query, divide your eye contact equally among all panel members. Taking a deep breath before speaking is also helpful in calming nerves.

It's a good idea to take a few notes as the interview day proceeds. Without them, you will forget key points by the time you get home. Don't let the notes become a distraction. For that reason, we recommend pen and paper, as an electronic screen tends to create a barrier between you and the other person. Spend most of your time making direct eye contact with the interviewer. Capture the name and title of everyone with whom you speak. Get their business card if possible. Jot down a few bullet points about the conversation with them.

Be aware that some companies use various standardized assessment tools to give additional insight into your interpersonal style or skills. You may be asked to take one or more of these tests. From the employer's perspective, these instruments are intended to help assess a candidate's creativity, problem-solving skills, fit with the job, and various other characteristics. Approach the assessment like you would any other interview question. Answer it honestly. From the results, you may learn something about yourself. The results may also help you refine your desired career goal and working environment.

Asking Questions

One of the best ways to distinguish yourself from other candidates is by asking great questions. By showing your curiosity in this way, you:

- Demonstrate that you've researched the company and have a sincere interest in it
- Highlight your intellectual reasoning and analytical skills
- Show that you are focused on what you can contribute to the company, rather than, "It's all about me."
- Get the chance to learn about things that are not obvious through research. Examples include company culture, career paths, and long-term company goals.

Be prepared with a set of questions before you arrive. Jot them down in your notebook in case you have a brain freeze in the moment. As much as possible, phrase your queries as "company-oriented" versus "self-oriented." You still get the information you want, but you have positioned yourself as genuinely interested in the company as opposed to having it be all about you.

For example, let's say you want to find out your potential career path. A self-oriented question might be phrased like this: "What would my career path be from this job?" To make the query company-focused, rephrase like this: "What are typical career paths in your company?" Similarly, if you want to find out about training opportunities, compare these questions:

- "What training will you provide me?"
- "What training does your company provide?" or "What is your educational reimbursement policy?"

If you put yourself in the company's shoes, which questions come across as more positive? It may seem minor, but anything you can do to tip the scale in your favor is worth doing.

Before leaving the premises, be sure to find out timing of the company's next steps. Ideally, this conversation will be with the hiring manager. It's fair to ask when they expect to make a decision. If you have other offers in hand, tell them when you will need to respond to the other employers so that you can consider a potential offer from this company as well.

The View from the Pros

Senior HR managers are a great source for advice on interviewing. They are experienced with a variety of interviewing techniques and are often very perceptive. Smart hiring managers use them as trusted partners and advisors throughout the process. When asked what advice she'd give young professionals on interviewing, Susan Penn, Vice President of HR, offered the following:

> "One of the most important suggestions I have to offer is to prepare. Know about the company and know your own strengths to the degree that you can give examples of your proficiencies. When in the interview, focus on conversing rather than reading off a list of your skills. Get away from corporate speak—that's a smoke screen that does not tell the company much about you personally. Be authentic.
>
> Pay attention to the interviewer's style so you can 'match' it. This assists in building a connection. Use these cues to connect, but do not get too relaxed.
>
> Listening and emotional intelligence will always stand out in an interview. If a candidate does not answer the question, but rather answers in practiced ways that seem not to match the specific question, I'll rephrase to get to the heart of the matter. If this happens more than once or twice, the interview is over (at least in my mind).
>
> So much depends on whether you 'click' or not. Often there's nothing you can do about this. Even though I've conducted over 3,000 interviews, it's clear to me that there are intangibles that we pick up about each other that occur under the surface.
>
> Last, even if you are not interested in the position, see it through until the end, even following up afterwards. Keep your energy up and positive throughout, and leave the interview feeling good about how you managed the interaction, whether you want the job or not."

Similarly, professional employment recruiters have seen it all in their years of working with job seekers and employers. Their clients are companies who hire them to help fill job openings. These open positions are typically, though not always, higher-level jobs or positions with very specific and hard-to-find skill requirements. Though it's unlikely you'll be contacted by one of these firms for an entry-level job, you can still learn from their experience working with senior employees.

Three of the experts we consulted for advice are current or former executive recruiters. Ken Schmitt, President of TurningPoint Executive Search, offers these suggestions for succeeding at interviews:

> "Focus on the 'Six BEs of Interviewing.' These are: BE prepared; BE a good listener; BE inquisitive; BE specific and cite real examples; BE energetic and enthusiastic; and BE yourself."

Megan Ahn, President of Accountants Direct, a search firm for financial professionals, recommends the following:

> "Personally, be prepared, on time, and humble. Professionally, take a sincere interest in the people you meet regardless of their title or position. Stay focused on the company and what they need to have accomplished. Companies hire people who can help them with work they need to get done. They really don't care to hear about your entire life. Companies hire when they have a need and want a person who is excited to get the job done."

Jeff Hastings, a former executive recruiter, gave us these suggestions:

> "Stick with the fundamentals and do your homework. Be prepared for the standard questions. Convince the employer that what you lack in experience and skill you will make up for in commitment and motivation. Do your homework and have smart questions to ask. Don't bother with clichéd answers to timeworn questions. And for Chrissakes, be on time in your best suit."

You might be surprised to discover that sometimes even executive-level people screw up on these basics. Jeff went on to offer this story:

> "One morning I got up before dawn to catch a flight to Los Angeles specifically to interview a candidate at an airline lounge. I called when she didn't show and asked where she was. She replied, 'It's raining outside so I don't want to drive all the way to the airport.' She didn't get the job."

Similarly, Ken shared this anecdote:

> "I was working on a search for a large, Midwest-based electronics firm. We were down to the final phase of the interviewing process. This candidate—a very senior, successful sales executive—simply had to meet with one final member of the executive team. Unfortunately, he thought it would be completely appropriate to interview with a wad of tobacco in his cheek. To make matters worse, he carried a soda can with him that he used as a spittoon! Needless to say, he did not get the job."

We're confident you'll perform much better than these two clueless candidates. Just do your homework, act professionally, treat everyone with kindness and respect, ask good questions, be open and honest with your answers, and you'll be fine. Show up even if it's raining and leave the spittoon at home.

After the Interview

Within 24 hours after the interview, you should follow up with thank-you notes to each person with whom you spoke. Email is fine. An additional snail mail note is a plus and is recommended if you really want the job. Tailor the note to the conversation you had with each individual. (This is where your notes come in handy.) A few sentences are all you need. If you write both an email and a snail mail note, make sure your content is different in each.

Wait a few days after your thank-you notes are received, and then send a LinkedIn® request to have your new contacts added to your professional network. These people will either be colleagues if you get the job or can be helpful in your ongoing search if not.

Almost all companies will ask for references, so be prepared with a list of people who have previously consented to be contacted. Be aware that many companies now conduct background checks, drug tests, and credit checks for potential employees. Expect that any claims you've made on your resume will be vetted, especially college degrees and formal work experience. Be sure your Facebook page puts you in the best light.

Receiving the News

Let's first deal with the bad news scenario. Should the company notify you that you weren't the candidate they selected, handle it gracefully and professionally. Rejection means nothing more than someone else had the edge over you. No more, no less. You're still an awesome candidate for a job somewhere, just not this one. Thank the hiring manager for his or her time.

Ask whether you could get some honest feedback on how you interviewed. Many people will be reluctant to do this, so don't be surprised if you simply receive some platitudes on what a difficult decision it was. Listen to any feedback dispassionately and don't be defensive. It's a real gift to get honest comments on your performance, even though some of it may be hard to hear. Learn from it and move on. It also wouldn't hurt to ask whether the hiring manager has any suggestions about where else you might send your resume, whether within the company or somewhere else. You never know where someone else's network might lead.

At some point in the process, you WILL receive a phone call with great news. A job offer! You may also be in the fortunate position of dealing with multiple offers. Which one should you choose? How do you negotiate the offer? Let's deal with those exciting questions next.

CHAPTER 13

NEGOTIATING AND CHOOSING

*"Choose a job you love and you'll never have
to work a day in your life."*
– CONFUCIUS

Now it gets fun! For the entire duration of your job search, power and control have resided with potential employers. You've been networking for weeks, searching for open positions, waiting for calls or emails, and have probably been rejected more than once. With one or more offers in hand, the game changes. Now, you are in the driver's seat and your future employer(s) are biting their corporate nails wondering whether you'll accept their offer.

Negotiating actually starts during the interview process. The more you impress people, and the better your skills, experience, and style fit with the company, the more they will want to hire you. Make sure you are paying attention to "buying signals" like these along the way:

- A question is preceded by the phrase, "Suppose you were to take this job..."
- The hiring manager or someone in HR queries you about salary or compensation needs.
- Someone in authority inquires when you would be able to come back for another round of interviews or when you would be able to start.
- Several people make overt statements about you being a "fit" or "match."

- You get introduced to people not officially included on the interview schedule, especially senior managers or direct co-workers.
- People are added to your interview schedule while you are there interviewing.
- One or more of the interviewers sound like they're "selling" the company, job, department, and working environment. The more people you hear this from, the more positive an indicator it is. While you're still in the building, hiring managers will sometimes do a brief check-in with early interviewers to gauge their reaction to you. If feedback is overwhelmingly positive, they may encourage the later interviewers to shift into selling mode. Be attentive to this.

If you notice any of the above, power has started to shift into your court. During the interviews, you can use these cues to your advantage by subtly laying the groundwork for what you are looking for in job title and job scope. The presence of these buying signals also makes it more likely that you will get asked about salary requirements while you're there, so be prepared for that conversation. (See below for some tips.)

General Guidelines

Early in your working career, the idea of negotiating with a potential employer is probably intimidating. It's easy to look at an offer, say, "Yippee!" accept, and be done with it. If you do this, you may be selling yourself short. Let's take a look at some general guidelines on how to approach a negotiation for a new job. We'll then dive into the details of several specific areas.

Rhonda Rhyne, former CEO and author of *The Bitch and the Glass Ceiling*, offers this set of suggestions:

1. **Role-play before you negotiate.** This can reduce anxiety, prepare you for a variety of responses, and increase your confidence.
2. **Research salary range prior to negotiating.** Since money does play a key factor in career satisfaction, it's important not to shortchange yourself.
3. **Set your own salary expectations.** Define a compensation range and set goals. Before negotiations commence, calculate the minimum amount you are willing to accept. If the offer doesn't

meet your minimum requirement and cannot be negotiated higher, consider passing on the offer. Also, don't adopt the mindset that whatever they offer is "good enough." If you accept the first offer, the "buyer" feels like they could have gotten you for less.

4. **Delay salary discussions as long as possible.** If you are employed, avoid stating your current salary as prospective employers frequently make offers based on your current pay. If you are asked your salary, try to deflect, state the range applicable to the position, and state you are confident the employer will make a fair and equitable offer. If you cannot get around the question, do not lie about your salary. Companies frequently ask for paystubs or W-2s.

5. **Be positive and understand practically everything is negotiable.** If you have an offer, they are interested in you. After researching the position and knowing your worth, you should enter negotiations with optimism and confidence that will help ensure successful negotiations.

6. **Make the negotiations into a collaborative, win-win, problem-solving exercise.** Framing the negotiations as a win-win situation, as compared to a competitive approach, is better received.

7. **For every concession you make, ask for something in return.** For example, if you are accepting a lower salary than requested, request a higher title and/or a shorter time until the next salary review.

8. **Take time to reflect on each offer before rejecting, asking for more, or accepting.** This will make you appear to be thoughtful, objective, and appreciative of your prospective employer's efforts.

Negotiating the Details

When an offer of employment arrives, it should contain the following features:

- A specific job title and description of duties
- The name and title of the person to whom you will report
- A specified salary
- A description of the benefits and other components of the compensation package

- A rough indication of desired start date
- A time frame in which you need to respond

If any of these are missing, go back immediately and get them clarified before the clock starts ticking on needing to decide.

Know with whom you will be negotiating. Speaking directly to the hiring manager is best. They are the ones feeling the pain of the open position, and they own the budget for it. Sometimes a company will have HR do the negotiating. If that's the case, do your best with them, but don't be afraid to call the hiring manager if your needs are not being met. Should you strike out with HR and decide to call the hiring manager, apologize for going to them directly. Then, tell the hiring manager you thought he or she would want to be informed about the impasse and that you need their help in resolving it.

The above bulleted items can all be negotiated. Let's talk about each one in turn.

Job Duties and Job Title

Many people do not think of job duties and job title as being negotiable. They are, to a degree. We recommend very carefully reviewing the list of job duties first. In some cases, there may be one or two duties not directly connected to the job that the company just needs to have land somewhere. They may not even have been mentioned to you in the interview process. For example, a receptionist could be tasked with doing some clerical accounting work. If you know you would be horrible at that task, it's better to say it up front, such as, "I notice there is some accounting work in here. Math is not one of my strengths. I'd be happy to take on other duties that aren't currently in the job description, but I think we both would be more satisfied if someone else were assigned this piece." Make sure to suggest other things not in the description that you would be willing to do. In this example, such tasks might include ordering supplies, making copies, staffing trade show booths, making coffee, or whatever.

Should you choose to negotiate the removal of certain job duties, be very careful. You are not looking to shirk duties; you are looking to set yourself up for success. You don't want to be perceived as a slacker from the get-go. If the job duty in question is core to this position, don't even try to negotiate it out. (If that's the case, just reject the job offer if you're unable or unwilling to do it.)

Even more important (and less common) is to negotiate for additional job duties. This is a fabulous way to be seen as a hard-working, ambitious contributor, even before you start the job. What is missing that you really want to do or learn? In what areas do you excel that aren't represented in the job description? For example, for an entry-level telesales position, see if you can represent the company at a trade show booth. That way, you can hone your in-person sales skills, and put yourself in a position to be considered for an in-person sales job when one opens up at the company. If you've added a substantial chunk of duties, your salary offer may even be raised! Again, be careful here. You don't want to end up with so much on your plate that you become overwhelmed.

Job titles are a bit trickier. You don't want to come off as egotistical and self-aggrandizing by asking for a title way beyond your duties, skills, and experience. On the other hand, sometimes companies (especially smaller and medium-sized firms) just don't do a good job with making titles accurate and descriptive. So, if you are given an offer with only the title "Assistant," it is totally appropriate to ask for it to be made more specific to Marketing Assistant, Sales and Marketing Assistant, Executive Assistant, or whatever else is appropriate. The same advice goes for Analyst, Supervisor, Lead, Manager, Intern or other generic-sounding descriptions. Remember that this title will be the one you put on your business cards and on the next version of your resume, so you want it to be accurate and impressive.

Name and Title of the Person to Whom You Will Report

For most people, your supervisor is one of the key determinants of happiness in your job. In fact, it's one of the more common reasons for leaving a position. While in a smaller company there may not be much flexibility, in a larger firm there may be some leeway into whom you report. For example, if there are several regions of the country for a telesales role, there may be an opening in more than one of them. If so, make sure you meet both managers during your interview process and request to report to the one you think would be the best fit.

Occasionally, there might be some flexibility on the level of organizational seniority of the person to whom the position will report. For example, an entry-level accounting job might report to a staff accountant, to the accounts payable manager, or to the controller. (For those who might not know, those roles above are listed in ascending order.) You want someone who has time to spend with you, from whom you can learn, and who you like. If your gut has a question mark about the person who will supervise you, probe gently whether there is any flexibility. Combining this discussion with expanding your job duties is a great way to pull this off.

Salary

Salary negotiations are a tricky dance. Jeff Hastings, a former executive recruiter, says, "The first person to mention a number in any negotiation loses." There's a degree of truth in this, as it is highly unlikely that you'll be offered more than what you indicate are your salary requirements. Sherri Petro recommends that you:

> "Know your ceiling and your floor. Think very carefully about what you can live with and what will make you miserable. I have found that if I have to talk myself into taking the offer, it is an ominous sign that this is not going to work out well."

If you are lucky, the salary range is in the job description. Other times, you can get an HR person to provide the position's salary range, as one component of their role is to screen out people early if they wouldn't take the job due to salary. If you know someone at the company (especially if it's a large firm), they may be able to tell you the salary range for that particular job. You can also try a Google search to find general salary ranges by job title. Note that salaries vary greatly by geography. Keep this in mind when you view these averages. For example, software engineers are paid much higher salaries in Silicon Valley than they would receive in Iowa, even if employed by the same company.

If pressed to come up with your salary requirements, you might try a line like this: "Based on my skills and relevant work experience, I think I would fit comfortably in the middle of your salary range for this position." Of course, if your skills are in high demand and you have extensive work experience, aim higher. Come across as reasonable, unemotional, and fact-based. Asking for a number that is at the very top of the salary range (or even above it) might result in no offer at all, especially if it's not consistent with what you bring to the party.

The hiring manager may not have as much flexibility with salary as you might think. Especially at larger firms, the salary ranges are generally well defined based on what other employers are paying for the same job in the area. Diane, a Vice President of HR, points out that, "Salaries may be capped, but sometimes things other than money can be negotiated. These include education, vacation, and other perks. Think creatively."

Beyond Salary

We'll assume here that you've finished your salary negotiation, and you got the best you could. Note, however, that you should not accept a job offer based on salary alone. If you're asked in the interview if you'd accept an offer at a certain salary, just say that it depends on the rest of the package.

As the negotiation continues after reaching closure on salary, you might say something like, "I recognize and appreciate that you did the best you could for me on the salary front. Can we discuss a few other things that will improve my satisfaction with the overall package, and my likelihood of accepting the job?"

To be successful at this, think in advance about what you want in addition to salary. Focus on what you can legitimately justify or on what would be a boon to your productivity. In any of these negotiations, your aim is for a win-win situation: you are happier and the company feels what you asked for is reasonable and not too costly to provide.

If you ask for too much, you look high maintenance. That could be a red flag for the company and you might lose a potential offer. If you come across as always wanting more, and neglect to emphasize how much you want the job, it will come across poorly. We recommend picking one or two things that are especially meaningful to you, and focusing on those.

You should negotiate only on items that the person on the other side of the table has the power to grant. Many benefit perks, for example, are standardized for all employees. Examples include educational reimbursement, gym membership, mileage reimbursement for business travel, and parking subsidies. Your chances of getting anything beyond what's offered to everyone else are pretty slim. Unless you have a clear and convincing case that you have a unique need, it's best not to bother. Instead, acquaint yourself with the standard offerings and factor those into the total compensation package.

Here is a list of potential items that may be negotiated beyond salary. They are ranked roughly according to degree of difficulty to obtain (easiest to hardest):

- **Work equipment:** Certain jobs require specialized tools and machines. A mechanical engineer, for example, may want a high-end workstation with particular computer-aided design (CAD) software. We've seen companies assign the decrepit old machines to the new kid. If you need specific equipment to be more productive, then say so. See if the company's budget will provide what you want. If not, and you've made a reasonable request, then that's a red flag. Look around to see what other equipment exists in the work setting. If you're a big Apple Mac fan and the office is PC-based, a request for a Mac is unlikely to be granted (and vice versa).

- If the position requires lots of driving, is a **company car** provided? A former roommate of Lauren's had an entry-level job as an insurance claims adjuster and a company car was part of the package. (Be careful what you wish for: she didn't love being 24 and driving a boring sedan that her grandparents might buy!)

- **Working hours**: Do you have preferences or requirements for when you arrive or depart work? Do you like to work out at lunch? If so, managers often have leeway to negotiate working hours with employees, as long as the job doesn't require that you be in your chair at prescribed times, like airline pilots, librarians, customer service reps, and so on. Probe the company's flexibility on this if it's important to you. Know that you may need to prove yourself before it's implemented.

- **Membership in industry groups and associations**: These usually have fees, so it's great to get company sponsorship. If these groups provide good visibility and learning opportunities for you in your career, shell out your own bucks even if the company won't.

- **Ability to occasionally work from home**: Be careful with this one. In the early months of your employment, you need a lot of face time in the office so that people get to know you and vice versa. If you have a horrendous commute and working from home would make a difference to your productivity, then perhaps it's worth making the request. Otherwise, we recommend you don't bring this up until you are fully trained and have proven your worth to the company.

- **Additional vacation time**: This falls into the category of "standard benefit item" discussed above, so it's generally not negotiable. However, if you have already booked a vacation in the future, you can sometimes get the company to advance you vacation time before you've earned it or let you take those days as unpaid time off. For example, very seldom will employers refuse to let someone take their pre-booked flight home to see their parents at the holidays.

- Request that your **first salary review** occur at six or nine months rather than the typical annual review. As with vacation time, the performance review process is standardized at many companies, so your chances of success may not be high. If you ended up with a salary on the low end of your expectations during that part of your negotiation, you could consider asking for an early review. Should you decide to do this, offer to tie the early review to a major achievement or milestone on your part. Don't expect that a company will make an exception to the salary review process without clear evidence that your performance warrants it.

When negotiating these elements of your package, the trick is to get what you want without sounding unreasonable. Don't forget that you will end up as an employee at one of the places you're negotiating with, so you want to leave everyone feeling good about the interactions.

Start Date

Once a company wants you, they are likely to somewhat flexible on when you start work. After all, if you are currently employed by another company, you will need to give at least two weeks' notice to your employer. Even if you are not employed, you can often negotiate to start in two or three weeks. If you have the cash, this is a fabulous time to take a vacation. You have your job, you won't get much vacation once you start, and you have no job-related worries hanging over your head on the trip. Go for it if you can!

Response Timing

Once a company has given you a job offer, they want you to respond quickly. This can be tricky, especially if you are in the late stages of talking to other companies and expect job offers from them soon. If that's the case, you can often buy an additional week or ten days to give a response. If you ask for more than that, they are understandably going to assume that their job is not your top choice. So, be careful. Notify the other companies you're talking to and tell them you have an offer in hand. Inform them when you'll need to respond so they will have an opportunity to finish their process and get you an offer if they want to pursue you.

Choosing

Deciding whether to accept an offer, or making a choice among multiple offers, requires a combination of skills. It starts with a clear knowledge of what you want. The work you did earlier in the search process now becomes invaluable in this regard. The actual choice involves a combination of analytical skills and gut instinct. We will focus mostly on the analysis part here, because that part we can teach.

However, do not neglect your gut in making your job decision. If you have a funny feeling about someone or something at a company, listen to it. You may want to probe further to see if you can identify why. Sometimes you can't quite put your finger on it, yet we'd still recommend listening to that voice. Diane, Vice President of HR, says that, "The jobs that worked out were the ones where I followed my instincts. I have taken two jobs in my career that were mistakes, both for reasons other than the position itself. In each case, my gut said, 'No,' but I did it anyway."

Similarly, if something feels like a fit but you can't pinpoint exactly why, listen to that feeling as well. Also, notice whether your energy and enthusiasm goes up when talking or thinking about a particular company or job. Factor the signals from your gut and emotions into the analytical model below.

Here's how to use the prioritized job criteria list you developed in Chapter 6 to assist you with your acceptance decision. Let's resurrect our fictional character Gloria to show you how to proceed. You may remember that Gloria's prioritized job criteria looked like this:

1. Sales role
2. Unlimited commission
3. Excellent training
4. Salary greater than $60,000
5. Opportunity for advancement

By definition, since these criteria are in priority order, they are not equally important. So, when evaluating particular job opportunities, Gloria needs to give each item a weighting according to its relative importance to her.

Gloria's criteria are listed from most important to least, so the value she assigns will be highest at the top and lower as she goes down the list. The sum of the total number of possible points is 100. After thinking about how important each item was to her, Gloria came up with the following allocations:

Criteria	Maximum score
Sales Role	40
Commission	25
Training	15
Salary	10
Advancement	10
Total score	100 points

Gloria has received offers for an entry-level sales position at Megacorp, Behemoth Bank, and Microcorp. She needs to choose one of these offers, or reject them all. Her percentage allocations become the maximum possible score for each of the criteria. So, a "perfect" job (and we know there's no such thing) would get 100 points. Gloria looked at each criterion and assigned a point score for each company, up to the maximum score she's allotted for each item. Here's how her ratings looked:

Criteria	Max Score	Megacorp	Behemoth Bank	Microcorp
Sales Role	40	40	40	25
Commission	25	20	15	25
Training	15	12	15	9
Salary	10	10	8	4
Advancement	10	6	8	10
Total score	100	88	86	73

This analysis gives a slight edge to Megacorp. The first thing to assess is whether an 88 or 86 is high enough to accept. We would certainly say so! (The decision is much harder if the best offer is say, a 70 out of 100.) Presuming her gut feelings are positive, Megacorp will be her choice. Given that Behemoth Bank is such a close second, Gloria might also try another round of negotiation with the bank to see whether they would be willing to tweak the package to put them over the top. Or, she may even go back to Megacorp, if she thinks that she has any additional wiggle room with them. If Gloria has been astutely reading the tea leaves, she'll have a reasonable feel as to what might be possible. Microcorp, on the other hand, clearly runs a distant third, so it probably isn't worth any further negotiations.

You Have a Job!

Savor the offer(s) you have received. It's a real testament to you when you find out that an employer values your skills and believes you'll be a great fit on the team. Weigh everything carefully and make the choice that speaks to your heart and your bank account. Happily, you only interviewed for positions that met your criteria. Assuming the interviews confirmed this and the compensation package is satisfactory, odds are good that the job is a good match for you. One of Lauren's 20-something career coaching clients offered this advice: "Go with your gut instinct. Don't overanalyze it. Just do it!" So, negotiate well and choose wisely.

CHAPTER 14

AFTER ACCEPTANCE

"Do not plan for ventures before finishing what's at hand."
– EURIPIDES

Congratulations, your quest is over and you'll be starting your new job soon! Take time to celebrate before you get really busy with your new work life. This chapter outlines several things to take care of shortly after accepting the new position. Once you start working, you will be so swamped with other stuff that it will be easy to forget the items below. We strongly recommend you finish these tasks before you start "drinking from the fire hose" at work.

Clean Up Loose Ends

If you have open offers from other companies, turn them down promptly. It's best to do this with a phone call. Avoid email. Thank the hiring manager once again for the opportunity. Should you know someone else who might be well qualified for the position you declined, offer to make a connection. Leave the other employers feeling good about you. It's not only a nice thing to do; you may be calling on them again in the future as a supplier, customer, or potential employee.

Inform Your Network

Many people helped you in your job search. Send a short email update with the details on your new position (including your new contact information) and thank people for their help. Offer to return the favor someday. For those people who were extremely helpful, set up a thank-you lunch or after-work libation. If you neglect this task, you may find that these people will be less enthusiastic about helping the next time around.

Update your LinkedIn® profile with your new role and where you will be working. As time goes on, remember to add new information about your experience and update your job title when you get promotions or new responsibilities.

You never know when you'll be looking for your next job. Keep in touch with key members of your network, especially with those who are well connected within industries and companies where you have an interest.

Understand Your Benefits

Your salary is the biggest piece of your compensation. However, you will be happy to discover that the benefits your new employer provides are worth a significant chunk of cash, too. Make sure you understand what the company offers so you can maximize the value you receive. If you can get a benefits summary prior to starting work, all the better. Then you can figure it out before you're buried in your new job. Generally, larger companies are able to fund more generous benefits packages than their much smaller brethren. Let's take a look at some of the common offerings in a good benefits package.

Health insurance: Coverage for medical care can be an extremely valuable benefit. If you've tried shopping for coverage on the individual market, you know what we mean. Increasingly, many employers share the cost with employees. Carefully review the documents provided and don't hesitate to ask someone in the Employee Benefits or HR department if you have questions. Some employers, particularly smaller companies, do not provide health insurance due to the cost. If you are in this situation, you may be eligible to continue coverage under your parents' policy. Check on this. In our opinion, it would be crazy to go without medical insurance. Many bankruptcies in the United States result from medical bills. If employer coverage is not available, investigate purchasing a policy on the individual market by looking at sites like **www.ehealthinsurance.com** or by talking with an insurance broker.

Dental insurance: These policies, obviously, cover care of your teeth. Procedures like teeth cleaning are often covered at little or no cost if you use in-network providers. Other dental work is covered at much lower out-of-pocket expense than you would pay on your own. If your employer does not provide coverage, you could consider buying an individual policy. Alternatively, you could crunch the numbers to determine whether to self-fund your dental work. If you are healthy and have a history of only requiring routine dental care, then taking a chance on paying out-of-pocket might make sense for a while. Find out how much an individual policy costs, and then ask your dentist for cost information on procedures you will likely need. Do the math and decide how much financial risk you are willing to take.

Disability insurance: This coverage will replace a portion of your income if you are no longer able to work due to a disability. What would you do if you were seriously injured in an accident and couldn't work for months? Would you be able to pay your bills? Disability coverage could significantly relieve the financial stress. Find out if the amount would be sufficient for your needs.

Life insurance: This pays your beneficiaries if you die. This is especially important if you have dependents. Some employers offer a group policy at favorable rates. If your employer offers coverage, compare it against policies available in the individual market to see what is most beneficial for your situation.

Vision coverage: If your employer offers full coverage for eye exams and contacts/glasses, great! Many, however, require that you pay a monthly premium and co-pay for services rendered, or don't offer vision coverage at all. Again, do the math. If your expected out-of-pocket costs with self-payment are greater than what you have to pay for the insurance, then it might be worth it to enroll in the vision plan.

Time off: Items in this category include vacation time, sick days, parental leave, and possibly time to volunteer on community service projects. If you're curious to see what your time off benefits are worth, multiply your hourly or daily pay rate times the allowed time off. Odds are, it's a pretty nice chunk of change. Use sick leave only when you're truly sick. You'll get a bad reputation if your sick day consumption always seems to fall on Mondays and Fridays. For vacations, employers generally prefer that you schedule time off as far in advance as possible so they can make plans to cover for you in your absence.

"401(k)" retirement plan: The name comes from the section of the Internal Revenue Code that provides the legal basis for them. 401(k) plans are employer-sponsored retirement vehicles that allow you to defer some of your compensation and with it, defer the current taxes that would have otherwise been due. Investment earnings generated inside the 401(k) are also tax deferred until the money is withdrawn. A 401(k) is a "defined contribution" plan where the eventual payout is not specified in advance. The future payout will depend on: (1) the total contributions from you and your employer; (2) the gains that accrue from the investments you select; and (3) the age at which you begin withdrawing money. In effect, the investment risk is on the employee, not the employer.

If your employer matches your 401(k) contributions, take the money! We'll say it again: This is FREE MONEY! Figure out a way to contribute as much as you can. At a minimum, contribute enough to capture the entire employer match. Of course, use common sense here. If you have a huge balance on your credit card with obscene interest payments, then postpone your 401(k) contributions until you have your spending under control. As you'll see below, starting NOW with your retirement savings will have a major impact on your life later on.

By the way, some employers offer "Roth 401(k)" programs as well. The contributions you make to a Roth 401(k) are on an after-tax basis. Withdrawals are generally tax-free at retirement, subject to certain conditions.

We strongly encourage you to familiarize yourself with the plan documents that govern any 401(k) program that's available to you. Though retirement may seem a long way off, we can promise you that money you save now will multiply dramatically over 35 to 40 years. Unless you want to depend on government programs like Social Security being there when you're retired, you need to realize that your standard of living in retirement will in large part be driven by what you save now. Don't avoid this.

Stock purchase plans: Many companies that have publicly traded stock offer the opportunity to purchase their stock at a discount. Some of these programs are handing you free money if you take advantage of them; others are less generous. Read the fine print carefully. Also, keep an eye on how much of your employer's stock you may be accumulating over time. You don't want to tie up too much of your financial net worth in your employer. Even great companies sometimes suffer major meltdowns in their stock. Talk to a financial advisor as appropriate.

Stock options: Your package may include options to purchase shares in the company over a period of time. High-tech companies are famous for offering options to attract top talent. Typically, these vest (mature) over a period of four years or so. Depending on the performance of the company, you could end up with a serious jackpot or nothing at all. Again, read the fine print carefully and discuss your questions with a financial advisor.

Pension plans: A "defined benefit" plan is a commitment by your employer to pay you a specified amount of money at your retirement. If you are fortunate enough to have one of these, your plan documents will spell out how many years you need to work to accrue the stated benefit. Many private employers no longer offer the defined benefit pensions that were so common 20 or 30 years ago. Many government entities, unionized companies, and some other organizations still offer them, but their numbers are dwindling due to cost pressures.

Other benefits: Depending on the company, you may see a variety of other services in your overall package. These may include gym discounts, tuition assistance, adoption assistance, employee assistance programs, and product discounts. Find out what's available, and be sure to take advantage of any that might benefit you.

Plan to Retire a Millionaire

How much do you think you need to invest now to retire a millionaire? The answer may shock you:

An investment of $4.25 per day beginning at age 20 can
yield a balance of more than $1,000,000 by age 70.

This example assumes an average 8% annual return in the stock market over the time period in question. (This is the approximate pre-tax historical long-term average stock market return, though results vary widely from year to year.)

Here's the real eye-opener: By waiting just a few years, the amount required to achieve the same result gets dramatically higher:

- $10/day at age 30 ($300/month)
- $23/day at age 40 ($690/month)
- $57/day at age 50 ($1,710/month)

While you're in your 20s, you have a huge financial advantage over your parents and grandparents and that is: TIME.

We'd like to acquaint you with a concept called the **time value of money**. Simply put, it is better to save money now than at some point in the future because it can be invested or earn compound interest over time. This is an extremely powerful idea, particularly when applied over many decades.

In the above example, by investing $4.25/day (or $125/month) starting at age 20 with an average annual 8% stock market return, you'd have about

$1,000,000 in 50 years. Here's the interesting thing: During this period, you would have invested only $75,000 ($125/month x 12 months/year x 50 years) to get this result. If you wait until age 30 your ending balance would drop from about $1 million to $436,376. By waiting those ten years, you lost out on over $550,000!

Start thinking for the very long term. Pondering retirement when it won't happen for 40 to 50 years is a difficult thing to do. However, we can assure you that this will be an essential component to your financial success. Your job will provide the income. Your challenge is to manage that money wisely so that it serves you and not the other way around.

Manage Your Finances

There's an old adage that "expenses rise to meet (or slightly exceed) income." Avoid stepping into this trap. Now that you're free of student poverty and have a steady inflow of cash, it'll be easy to have your expenses overwhelm your income if you're not careful.

There's another reason why you should be paying attention to your cash flow. We hesitate to point this out while you're basking in the warm afterglow of gainful employment, but you ought to think about what would happen if your wonderful new paycheck suddenly vanished. If business turns bad and the company needs to do layoffs, the newer employees are often the first to be shown the door. It's also not unusual for companies to be acquired by larger firms. In Lauren's corporate career, this happened four times. That can also mean layoffs.

These are only a few scenarios that may result in the loss of your paycheck. You may or may not see it coming. Jim's brother David got sacked when a significant chunk of his department was outsourced to India in a corporate cost-cutting move. David is now happily hugging those big bags of cash that he wisely accumulated during the fat-paycheck years as he ponders his next career move. You should be similarly prepared.

So, here are some tips to get started off on the right financial footing:

- **Always save at least 10% of your gross income.** Set it up with the bank to automatically transfer this amount to savings the moment your paycheck is deposited. (Some people call this "paying yourself first.") Build up a three to six month emergency fund to use in the event of job loss or unexpected financial surprises (think major car repair, medical expense, and so on).
- **Avoid debt, especially debt used to finance "stuff."** Consumer items nearly always depreciate (lose value) to be worth close to

nothing in fairly short order. Have a garage sale and you'll see what we mean. Save up and pay cash.

- **Always pay your credit cards in full every month**. Credit card debt is notoriously expensive. Once you start carrying a balance, it is very difficult to dig out of that hole.

- **Establish a budget and stick to it.** You'll find that the things you "need" to survive are pretty limited. These items include food, shelter, insurance, transportation, and basic clothing. Everything else falls into the "want" category. Pay for your "needs" first and fund the "wants" with what's left.

- **Avoid paying full retail price for ANYTHING!** It's almost always possible to acquire something for less than the price you see at first. Learn how to play the game to get the best deal. Not only is it fun, it will also put a bunch of money back in your pocket.

- As you build up savings, **learn to invest for the future**. Continuously educate yourself about personal finance. The bigger your cash pile, the greater freedom you'll have to do what you want with your life.

- **Know the role you want money to play in your life.** We all have some kind of philosophy about money, whether consciously formed or not. Our parents, spiritual upbringing, friends, and the media all influence that view. Thinking about this topic proactively will enable you to frame your philosophy about money, how you want to accumulate it, and how you want to spend it.

If you're interested in learning more, we'll give a shameless plug here for Jim's book, *From Ramen to Riches: Building Wealth in Your 20s*. It covers these topics, and more, in a way that is accessible to those who might not naturally gravitate to the subject of money.

Paying attention to your finances will help you get off to a good start. The income from your job will provide you with the resources you'll need to live your life as you want. Learn how to maximize the value of that inbound cash. Remember, it doesn't matter how much you make, it matters how much you keep.

CHAPTER 15

YOUR FIRST FEW MONTHS ON THE JOB

*"Even a mosquito doesn't get a pat on the back
until he's well into his work."*
– ANONYMOUS

Expect a roller coaster ride at work the first several weeks. You'll need to figure out how to do your job. And, you also have to deal with the nuts and bolts of navigating around a new environment, getting to know your colleagues, and determining what makes the place tick. Most people give a new employee a great deal of slack. They've all been there too and know what it feels like to be the new kid. They'll expect you to make a few newcomer mistakes. Your colleagues will initially be supportive if you are clueless about how things work. So relax.

At the same time, you can help yourself by working hard to ensure this period is as short as possible. Making a good initial impression and scoring some early wins will go a long way towards earning you goodwill from your co-workers and managers. Let's take a look at some ideas that will help.

Manage Yourself

The first few months of a new job will likely be the most stressful. You're new, you're learning, you have a lot of stuff coming at you, and there will be times when you feel completely incompetent. This is normal. Don't worry; it will get better soon enough.

You can help yourself through this period by taking care of yourself both physically and mentally. Eat well to avoid energy swings. Avoid junk food and sugary beverages. Bring healthy mid-morning and mid-afternoon snacks to work.

Vigorous exercise is a great way to burn off stress. Pick a regular time to work out and stick to it. Consider walking or bicycling to work if that is a viable option.

Manage your after-work life to ensure you are well rested when it's time for work in the morning. Keep an eye on your work hours to ensure you're keeping a sustainable pace. The work will always be there. Learn how to manage the tasks on your plate at work so that you still have a life outside the company.

Get to Know the People

Your success at work will be driven by your ability to perform and your skill at working with others. You may not like it, but office politics exist whenever there are two or more people in an organization. Don't ignore this part of the equation.

Focus on learning names and something personal about each person. Study the LinkedIn® profiles of everyone you connected with at the company following the interview process. Make 30-minute appointments with each individual with whom you will be working closely. Find out what they do, how you will work together, and how you can help and support each other. Connect via LinkedIn® to anyone you haven't already added to your network.

Get copies of organization charts to help you understand how the pieces fit together and who holds which roles. Figure out who has power and influence. You can often accomplish your goals through them. Avoid saboteurs and gossips. Be friendly, but stay off their radar screens.

By the way, just because someone's name is at or near the top of a department organization chart doesn't necessarily mean that person has power and influence. Carefully observe how people behave. Who gets things done? Who knows what's going on? Who is respected? Who do people listen to in meetings? These are all good clues.

Find a mentor to help you navigate the corporate politics, remove roadblocks, and coach you how to succeed in your work environment. Look for someone who is knowledgeable and well respected. Listen to their coaching and feedback. Be respectful of their time. They have jobs to do, too. Figure out how to help them in return.

Meet with customers or clients early on. They may be internal to the organization or external. If it's not clear, then figure out who is the main beneficiary of your work output and treat them as you would a paying external customer. Find out their expectations. Mutually agree with your customers and manager on how you will be measured against those expectations. By defining this up front, you'll know where to focus your efforts and avoid unpleasant surprises at performance review time.

Learn Your Job

Make sure someone explains what you're supposed to do and how. This may sound obvious, but you'd be surprised how frequently poor communication or lack of training gets in the way of successful performance. Reserve time with your manager or someone he or she designates to describe your responsibilities and how your performance will be measured. A good manager will also prepare a written document to outline this for you. If that doesn't happen, take the initiative to do it yourself and send it to your boss to confirm you each have the same understanding.

Take notes during conversations with those who are helping you learn your job. Ask questions if anything isn't clear. Only ask the same question once. Batch your questions to be respectful of others' time. You'll quickly get the cold shoulder if you're constantly interrupting someone, especially if they've already answered that question. Get the bigger picture of how your work fits into the whole. Understand why your position exists and why the job is important to the organization.

Make a Good Impression

Your mother was right about a few things, especially with regards to behavior towards others. Treat everyone with kindness and respect—even the jerks. As Jim's grandmother used to say, "You attract more flies with honey than vinegar." (We're not exactly sure why one would want to attract flies in the first place, but the analogy is useful.) You will definitely run into people you don't like. Figure out how to deal with them so that you can get your job done without a lot of drama.

Everyone gets a honeymoon period at the beginning. Use that to your advantage. Look for early, small wins. Show up at work a bit earlier than expected. Under promise and over deliver—people will always be impressed if you get things done a bit faster and better than expected. If you don't have enough to do, ask for more! Volunteer for special projects and committees. Be pleasant, upbeat, and agreeable, even when you don't feel that way. Respectfully state your opinion in meetings. Fully support team decisions, even if you didn't initially agree with a particular course of action. Help others succeed. Megan Ahn, the executive recruiter, suggests that you:

"Stay focused early on doing a great job at anything you do professionally. Remember that every successful executive started someplace. They built up their experience, education, and skills and along the way discovered their strengths. Very few people know at age 20 what they will be doing professionally at age 40. A cheerful, positive attitude and desire to do a great job at everything you do will offer you the most options."

Similarly, never miss a deadline. The halo over your head will tarnish quickly if you don't meet a commitment. Work late if necessary to deliver what you promised. If it becomes clear that you won't be able to meet a due date, inform everyone who needs to know well in advance so that the team can work out a Plan B. Observe the hours worked by others. There will be a standard that you want to exceed, not just meet. Unless your boss is a total workaholic, it's not a bad idea to regularly arrive before he or she does.

Make yourself indispensible. Earn a reputation as someone who knows what they are doing and can be counted on to make things happen. Not only will this help at performance review time, it'll also greatly reduce the odds that you get laid off if business turns down. Kim Box, former Hewlett-Packard Vice President, says,

"Remember that you are 'interviewing every day' by your actions. How you perform in your current position sets you up for your next position. Take it seriously, work hard, and get the intended results. Hard work without results is meaningless."

This should be obvious, but answer the phone when it rings and respond to email promptly. A few members of our expert panel commented that 20-something employees are more likely to respond to text messages than other forms of communication. Be warned that ignoring a ringing phone and neglecting email are considered highly unprofessional. Members of your generation may expect to handle the bulk of their communications via texting. Older generations do not. In particular, ignoring any form of customer communications is unforgivable, whether it comes by phone, email, fax, snail mail, text, or pony express. One suggestion: Ask people their preferred mode of communication, and then use that form whenever possible.

Finally, make people laugh! Work can sometimes be stressful. A bit of fun and levity improves morale and productivity. We're not suggesting you try to become the office jokester if that's not who you are. Rather, think about how to make work life a bit nicer for those around you. Your efforts will make things more pleasant for you in return.

Manage Up

One of your jobs is to make your boss look good and be successful. Take the time to understand your manager's priorities. Know how your work fits into those. Mutually agree on job responsibilities, priorities, and deadlines. Cláudia Schwartz, Principal at HR Results, said that her biggest career mistake was,

> "Not asking more open-ended, insight-provoking, constructive questions to help my managers clearly define what was expected of me. Since conflict comes from a gap in expectations, I could have been more effective in getting my employers to describe their definition of success and to stick to that shared vision."

Be positive and upbeat, but don't be a "suck up." Strive to be a low-maintenance employee. Remember the "Pareto Principle" (also called the "80/20 rule"). As former corporate managers, we can tell you that 20% of the employees took up 80% of our time. You don't want to be one of those 20%. On the positive side, 20% of the employees were truly high performers. You do want to be one of those!

Keep your manager in the loop. A surprise, especially a negative one, is the last thing your manager wants. Make sure your manager is informed about what's going on, both good and bad. At the same time, recognize that your supervisor is very busy, so use judgment on how often you do this. If you're unsure, check in occasionally to ensure you're both in alignment. Solicit regular, but not too frequent, feedback.

If someone compliments you in an email, don't hesitate to forward it to your boss if he or she hasn't been copied. Keep an email folder for accomplishments and compliments. This will be useful at performance review time.

One of the young professionals that Lauren coached through her job search reported that, "My biggest surprise about the world of work was the lack of guidance about career paths, how to do your job, training, and so on." If your manager does not attend to these important tasks, then you need to take the initiative. Do your homework and come prepared with an outline of what you'd like to do, ask your manager's advice and suggestions, and gain his or her support in proceeding. Remember to position the conversation as a discussion on how you can make the best possible contribution to the company. From there, you should be able to get the training and guidance that you want.

Manage Down

Even in an entry-level professional role, you may still have people who report to you, whether formally or not. For example, you may lead a team of peers to bring a project to completion. Perhaps members of other groups provide services to you or you have shared administrative support staff in your department.

When you're in a position of authority, use that power wisely. Be respectful of others' workloads. The tasks they are performing for you may only be a small subset of their jobs. While your requests may seem high priority to you, they may not be to the other person.

Make an effort to understand what else they are handling. Work with them to clarify mutual goals, including timeframes. Always tell someone the "why" when you are assigning a task. Explicitly agree on scope, priority, and deadlines. Set milestone check-in points. Summarize your agreement in an email to ensure you're both on the same page. As time progresses, check in at agreed-upon intervals and take action if things are going significantly off-track. Always say "please" and "thank you." Acknowledge a job well done and copy the appropriate manager(s). Celebrate successes with all involved.

Treat administrative staff with respect. They are professionals, too. An administrative assistant is potentially supporting dozens of other employees. Recognize that requests coming from his or her direct manager will take priority over everything else, including anything you may need. One final tip: Good administrative assistants are sometimes among the most powerful people in the office, particularly if they report to a senior manager. You'd be shooting yourself in the foot by getting on the bad side of someone like that. They are also great sources of information!

Manage Sideways

You'll quickly discover that having influence with your peers results in positive benefits to life at work. Your peer group may be people in your own department or in others. It'll be easy to figure out who some of these folks are. Others will be tougher. The obvious ones will be people in your department with the same job title. You'll find others with similar educational background and years of work experience in departments elsewhere in the organization.

Get to know these people. Go to lunch with colleagues. Initiate if they don't ask. Go out socially from time to time if you get invited. (Though remember these are work colleagues and not college buddies. Be careful to not over imbibe. Don't say or do anything that could reflect badly on you back at the office.) Invite peers from other departments to social gatherings, as appropriate.

Do small favors for people. Your helpfulness will generate goodwill and make people more likely to help you in the future. Befriend well-respected peers. Voice your opinion, listen to others, and help with coming to consensus. Once the team has decided on a course of action, even if you are overruled, support that decision gracefully. For team projects, get mutual agreement on scope, priority, roles, and deadlines. Always meet your commitments. Trust, but verify, that others are doing their part. Apply what you learned on team projects in college. The tactics that worked there will carry forward to a professional work environment.

Get Connected in Your Industry

After you get settled in, consider joining the local chapters of professional organizations whose members are in your specialty or industry. These groups host seminars and meetings that help you stay abreast of new developments. Also, they generally offer networking events that present an opportunity to meet others in your industry or profession.

Your networking doesn't end once you become employed. On the contrary, once you have a regular professional paycheck, your credibility rises with industry peers. Get to know people from a broad mix of relevant companies in similar or related fields. Connect via LinkedIn®. You never know when you'll be looking for your next job. As you now know, a robust network will be a tremendous help when that time comes.

You should also be prepared for a role reversal. As an employed professional, you may begin receiving queries from others who are looking for a job. Do what you can to help. It's good karma and is a nice way to repay all those who helped you during your quest for a job.

CHAPTER 16

SUMMARY AND CHECKLIST

"The true way to render ourselves happy is to
love our work and find in it our pleasure."
— FRANÇOISE DE MOTTEVILLE

With sustained effort and a good plan, you will find a job. Even better, having done the work in this book, you will find a job that matches your skills, interests, and experience. There are thousands of jobs out there, especially at entry level and early career. In this book, you learned how to find them.

Your mindset needs to be that this is possible. And why not? You have unique skills to contribute to the world. You now have a good toolkit for identifying your skills most applicable to the working world and packaging them in a compelling way. Finding a job takes introspection, initiative, and getting out there with your message. It takes effort and sometimes patience. Keep in mind why it's worth it. The prize is a job you love that uses your talents, allows you to grow and learn, and affords you an ever-improving lifestyle.

In this chapter, we've noted the key points and action items from each of the earlier chapters. We hope you find this to be a useful reference as you proceed with your job search.

The Big Picture (Chapters 1, 2, 3, and 4)

☐ To conduct a successful job search: know that you need to complete a rigorous self-assessment, find your passion, clearly explain and leverage your experience, identify your skills, build a strong network, master the search process, and have the right attitude.

☐ Construct a Life Vision to sketch out what you'd like your life to look like in the next several years. This compelling narrative paints a picture of your life when your goals and dreams have been fulfilled and you're living in a way that's consistent with your values. Completion of a Life Vision will help focus your actions for the upcoming job search.

☐ Develop a career strategy to guide your search. This high-level plan outlines your anticipated career direction, tentative timeline, key milestones, and things you know you want to learn and accomplish.

☐ Understand the job search process before you begin. Be aware that you will likely go through several steps more than once. You'll also be at different stages of the process on different opportunities, at the same time.

Self-Assessment (Chapter 5)

☐ Conduct a rigorous self-assessment to identify what you're good at, where your passions lie, and what you care about. This self-knowledge will help distinguish you from the majority of job seekers of any age.

☐ Identify your values. Values are the deep, enduring beliefs that you hold most closely to your heart. Values guide your ethics and behavior. They are crucial to feeling whole. The organization you work for will also hold a set of values. The values a company exhibits must be in alignment with your own for the job to be a good match.

☐ What are you passionate about? In the context of finding a great job, we are referring to the things you love doing with your time and care deeply about. Take the time to be introspective about what drives you. That effort will set you on a career and life path that brings you joy along the way.

☐ Skills relevant to an employer can be separated into two categories. The first for you to identify are considered the technical or "hard" skills you need to perform a particular job or task. Hard skills typically are more narrowly focused on a particular job description. The second set of skills to compile highlight your "soft" skills, such as leadership ability, communications skills, and so on. Soft skills can be applied across a variety of industries or situations.

☐ When thinking about finding a job you love, your life and work experiences are key components. Formal and informal jobs, extracurricular activities, sports, and hobbies are all relevant. What do all your experiences and activities have in common? What are the key themes? What aspects about these things do you like and why?

☐ Based on the above self-assessment, determine one or two possible role and industry combinations you will explore further.

Your Job Criteria (Chapter 6)

☐ Identify criteria for your ideal job to greatly enhance the probability that you'll find a position you want. These criteria will help you develop questions to ask during informational and formal interviews. They will also be the benchmark against which you'll evaluate job possibilities and offers.

☐ "Must-have criteria" will be a set of characteristics that must exist for you to even consider a particular job. Know your showstoppers in advance so you can rule out some opportunities before wasting more than a moment of your time.

☐ Rank your criteria from most to least important to clarify which characteristics have the most value to you.

☐ Use your prioritized job criteria frequently in the job search process. It'll be especially handy when networking, doing informational interviews, preparing for formal interviews, and evaluating job offers.

Your Resume (Chapter 7)

☐ Your resume is the presentation of yourself to the world of work. It is a crisp and clear description of who you are and what you bring to a potential employer. A well-constructed document is virtually a necessity to pass the first screening test.

☐ Highlight your skills, experience, and results with action verbs to ensure your resume sparkles with energy.

☐ Liberally sprinkle relevant keywords throughout the resume. These terms help corporate recruiters (people and computers) select the best possible matches. Include keywords for industry, functional, job-specific, and other competencies.

☐ Use the job objective section to describe in one sentence the position you're after. Be specific about what you want.

☐ Highlight work or other relevant activities that a potential employer may find applicable to the job in question in the experience section. Convey what you have done and what you can do. For every prior job, summarize your role and responsibilities. Follow that with three to five bullet points that highlight your accomplishments in a specific, results-oriented, and measurable way. Use numbers and percentages to add to the positive impression you are creating.

☐ The education component of your resume includes the name of the university, degree obtained, concentration, and year of graduation. Highlight any academic honors received and relevant club memberships, and anything else that helps you stand out from the crowd.

☐ Send a well-written cover email or letter along with your resume. This letter gives your resume context and relevance. Highlight some especially salient points for the specific position.

It's All About Your Network (Chapter 8)

☐ The vast majority (70-90%) of jobs are secured through networking. Spend job search time proportionally to this statistic.

☐ When building your professional network, the key to success is "who you can get to know," not necessarily who you know right now.

☐ For purpose of a job search, your network is the set of people you know combined with the set of people they know, and the set of people they in turn know. Often one of these second or third level connections will be your ticket to the dream job interview. Reach out to them.

☐ LinkedIn® is a terrific job search resource. Think of it as a social network with a focus on issues relating to business, careers, and job search. Leverage its capabilities.

Informational Interviewing (Chapter 9)

☐ Use informational interviews to gather information and garner introductions, rather than asking about specific job openings.

☐ Conduct informational interviews to learn about a certain industry, get to know what a particular job is like, practice interviewing skills, and obtain introductions to people who may be able to lead you forward in your search.

☐ Search LinkedIn® and your professional network to locate names of individuals to interview.

☐ Arrive on time with a well-prepared set of questions. Respect the agreed-to time limit. Always ask, "Who else do you recommend I have an informational interview with to learn more about this industry (or job)?"

☐ At an informational interview, don't ask about any open jobs at their company or others. The person you are speaking with will volunteer this information if they know of any available jobs and have been impressed by you.

Target Company List (Chapter 10)

☐ A target company list is a set of potential employers in the industry (or industries) in which you have an interest. These firms meet the job criteria you've outlined and have employees in the job title you want. Discover these companies through research, word-of-mouth, and informational interviews.

☐ Use your target list to help you focus your search on companies that meet pre-determined criteria. It'll also help you leverage your network more effectively.

☐ Apply each of your objective criteria against information available from public research sources. Typical forms of objective data include company size (revenues or employees), geographic location, and benefit offerings.

☐ Subjective criteria such as "a great place to work" or "lives up to its own corporate values" also factor into a decision to add or remove a company from the target list. Assess these criteria in conversations with people in your network, by reading media articles about the company, or simply by gut feel.

Sustaining Your Search (Chapter 11)

☐ Spend enough time on your search to sustain forward momentum while allowing yourself time to replenish your energy.

☐ Once you have completed your self-assessment, job criteria, and resume, about 80% of your time should be spent on informational interviews and networking. Get out there and spend time with people who can help you find your next job!

☐ Create some rewards and reinforcement to help you sustain your search. Tie them to the completion of specific activities.

☐ Hang out with other job searchers who are positive and focused. The attitudes of those around you are infectious.

☐ There's no good or bad time of the year to get hired. You are looking for only one job and that could happen at any time.

Interviewing (Chapter 12)

☐ The first step in the interview process is often a phone screen. When you get to this point, your odds have improved considerably. Offer crisp, direct answers to the questions you're asked. Avoid drilling down into lots of detail unless they probe further. Be honest and forthright always, and acknowledge when you aren't experienced in a certain area.

☐ Prepare for every formal interview the same way you prepare for a university exam. Learn everything you can about the company and the job in advance so that you can arrive prepared, knowledgeable, and engaged.

☐ The minute you walk in the door, put on your game face. Assume that everything you say and do will be observed and assessed until the time you leave the building.

☐ Remember that you are also being interviewed if you get taken to lunch. While the setting may be informal and relaxed, you are still being evaluated. Use lunch as an occasion to highlight your interpersonal skills.

☐ Be prepared for open-ended or behavioral questions that ask you to come up with actual experiences that highlight the skill being evaluated.

☐ Pay attention to your body language in every conversation. Lean slightly forward in the chair. Maintain eye contact. Nod occasionally when the other person is speaking to acknowledge that you've heard and understand. And don't forget to smile once in a while!

☐ Take a few notes as the interview day proceeds. Without them, you will forget key points by the time you get home. However, don't let this become a distraction. Be sure to spend most of your time making direct eye contact with the other person.

☐ Come prepared with a set of questions before you arrive. Jot them down in your notebook in case you have a brain freeze in the moment.

☐ Within 24 hours after the interview, follow up with email thank-you notes to each person with whom you spoke. Tailor the note to the conversation you had with each individual. Reiterate your interest in the company and job.

Negotiating and Choosing (Chapter 13)

☐ Negotiating actually starts during the interview process. The more you impress people, and the better your skills, experience, and style fit with the company, the more they will want to hire you. Make sure you pay attention to buying signals along the way.

☐ With one or more offers in hand, power shifts a bit from the employer to you. The greatest leverage you'll have is the time right before you accept an offer.

☐ Delay salary discussions as long as possible. The person who mentions a number first starts out with the weaker hand.

☐ Many things are somewhat negotiable, though some companies have more flexibility than others.

☐ The trick is to get what you want without being high-maintenance or sounding unreasonable. Don't forget that you will end up as an employee at one of these companies, so leave everyone feeling good about the interactions.

☐ Use the ideal job criteria you created at the beginning of your search to help you choose among several competing offers. Look at the objective criteria analytically and then let your gut weigh in on the intangibles.

After Acceptance (Chapter 14)

☐ If you have open offers from other companies, turn them down promptly, gracefully, and professionally.

☐ Many people helped you in your job search. Take the time now to send a short email update with the details on your new position and thank people for their help. Offer to return the favor someday.

☐ You will be happy to discover that the benefits your new employer provides are worth a significant chunk of cash. Make sure you understand what the company offers so you can maximize the value you receive.

☐ Develop a plan to manage your finances. There's an old adage that "expenses rise to meet (or slightly exceed) income." Avoid stepping into this trap.

Your First Few Months on the Job (Chapter 15)

☐ Most people give a new employee a great deal of slack. They've all been there too and know what it feels like to be the new kid. They'll expect you to make a few newcomer mistakes, so relax.

☐ The first few months of a new job will likely be the most stressful. Help yourself through this period by taking care of yourself both physically and mentally.

☐ Office politics exist whenever there are two or more people in an organization. Be cognizant of this part of the equation.

☐ Find a mentor to help you navigate the corporate politics, remove roadblocks, and coach you on how to succeed in your work environment.

☐ Make sure someone explains what you're supposed to do and how. You'd be surprised how frequently poor communication, lack of training, and unclear expectations get in the way of successful performance.

☐ Look for early, small wins. Show up at work a bit earlier than expected. Under promise and over deliver—people will always be impressed if you get things done a bit faster and better than expected. Make yourself indispensible.

☐ Answer the phone when it rings and respond to email promptly.

☐ Make your boss look good and be successful. Take the time to understand your manager's priorities. Know how your work fits into those. Be positive and upbeat, but not a "suck up."

☐ When you're in a position of authority, use that power wisely. Be respectful of others' workloads.

☐ After you get settled in, consider joining the local chapters of professional organizations whose members are in your line of specialty and/or industry.

As you read through the checklist, review the relevant concepts in the chapters listed if you are not clear on what needs to happen. Remember that you may find yourself going through various parts of the process at different times while juggling multiple opportunities. Follow the process, modify it as necessary, stay well organized, and it'll go fine.

A final suggestion: One of the best ways to improve your forward momentum is to choose three things that you'd like to do right now to move your job search forward. Then, tell three people what these things are and by when you want to have them accomplished. Ask them hold you accountable for getting these tasks done. If three people you value highly are going to ask you whether you met your commitments, you're much more likely to make those things happen. Repeat as necessary.

To Your Success!

Embarking on a job search is one of the most important tasks of your professional life. Done well, it will set you on a path to a career that ignites your passions, aligns with your values, and pays a salary that supports the life you want to live. You will meet many great people, some of whom may end up as lifelong friends and colleagues. And, you will use these job search skills many times during your career.

Be prepared for the occasional challenges you'll face along the way. Though you can't control the timing of when things will happen, you can manage your attitude and approach in a way that lets you ride out the bumps. Every job search eventually ends. We're confident yours will result in a job you love. We wish you all the best in your quest.

About the Authors

LAUREN TANNY is founder and CEO of The Tannywood Group, Inc., a consulting company focused on sparking company growth through leadership development, work force reinvigoration, and innovative new strategies. In addition to her own company, Lauren has run a venture-backed start-up and a business unit of a $200-million publicly traded software company. With an MBA from the Stanford Graduate School of Business, she is also a *magna cum laude* graduate of the third class of women at Dartmouth College.

JIM WOOD is a 25-year veteran of the high-tech industry, having held software engineering, information technology management, and business strategy management positions. His first book, *From Ramen to Riches: Building Wealth in Your 20s*, is a popular guide for 20-somethings who are looking to get a grip on managing their money. Jim has appeared on numerous local and national media programs, including PBS television's *Nightly Business Report*. He is a *summa cum laude* graduate of Boston University and also holds a master's degree in Engineering Management from Stanford University.

RESOURCES

For additional job search resources, please visit our website at:

www.tannywood.com/resources/career-decisions

* * * * *

For more information and updates on the
"From Ramen to Riches" series, please visit:

www.fromramentoriches.com

* * * * *

Follow us on Twitter at:

www.twitter.com/fromramentorich

* * * * *

And on Facebook at:

www.facebook.com/fromramentoriches

CPSIA information can be obtained at www.ICGtesting.com
Printed in the USA
LVOW121821041212

310065LV00005BA/77/P